The

Way

I

Walk

To Ann, all grace and blessings to you

The

Way

I

Walk

From Tugboat to Transplant

Cathy Cathy Cuenin

First Arrow Publishing – Suquamish Washington

for Loren, of course

PREFACE

This book began as I was writing short stories about our family's early years in Alaska, tales I want to leave for my granddaughter, Clara. Many memories of our young, adventuresome family at sea and in the wilderness fill my heart; I want Clara to know my stories, and I know I may not be here to tell them to her.

While writing, more recent events of disappointment and healing kept bubbling to the surface, making their way to pen and paper—the kind of challenges we all face at some time. I have strung the old and new stories together, alternating beads on the thread of my life. They create a joyful and painful dance, one of love and loss. I believe that each of us lives a life worth a novel, story, or poem, though not every one of us gets around to writing it down.

These stories cover a span of nearly forty years. From early adventures in the precious rainforest of Southeast Alaska, to more recent adventures of disease and miracles, these tales of *then* and *now* are snapshots of a life I have cherished. This is a memoir. These stories are accurate to the best of my memory, with a name change here and there. I invite you into the intimacy of my life and hope my stories tap something universal in you, something to inspire your living and dying.

ACKNOWLEDGEMENTS

Putting together this book could not have happened without the guidance and support of my writing teacher, friend, and first editor, Carmi Soifer. Time and again, Carmi encouraged me to continue when I felt ready to put this project to bed for one reason or another. Thank you, Carmi. And to my husband, Loren Gerhard, who has patiently encouraged me to write for years, since long before this memoir was conceived, I am immensely grateful.

1. OFF TO ALASKA—*Then*

"Oh for heaven's sake, just get a whole roll of wax paper, line your shower with it, turn on the cold water, and get in with your clothes on." This was my friend Chava trying to cheer me up when I was desperately homesick for Southeast Alaska. It was after we'd been in Southeast long enough to call it home, to fall in love with the place. At the time, we were spending a few years living "outside," in the Lower 48. When referring to Alaska, she failed to comment on the majestic, towering mountains with mist clinging to their steep slopes or to the deep blue waters. She was referring to the rain, the ever-present rain. And to the gray, gray sky. Chava and I had met twelve years earlier, sleeping beside each other on the back deck of the ferry when we moved north to Alaska.

***

Loren and I had just gotten married and were living in Seattle as I finished up nursing school. We were both twenty-four, and he had a passion for everything to do with boats. We would often find our way to the shores of Lake Union, watching the tugboats motor by. We imagined ourselves living aboard one of those old wooden boats with beautiful lines, the curving bulwarks reaching from one end to the other. I didn't have a clue then that one end was the bow and one was the stern. Front to back, they looked romantic to me. Now I know bow and stern, just as I know starboard and port. I even know the bathroom is the head.

With such romantic and adventuresome daydreams in mind, when I finished nursing school, I wrote to a hospital in Juneau, Alaska, the state capital, and one in New Orleans, looking for work. When the hospital in Juneau wrote back, offering me a job, I took it. "Well, okay," Loren said, "we better go check it out."

We set sail soon after, aboard the Alaska Marine Highway Vessel, *Columbia*, at the time the newest member of the fleet. One of the state's "Blue Canoes," the *Columbia* traveled up and down the inside passage, a route that wove through the islands off the Pacific Coast of Washington, British Columbia, and Alaska. It carried nearly six hundred passengers and two decks' worth of cars, trucks, RVs, boats, and animals with destinations all over Alaska. Riding the ferry, we were using Alaska's highway system. The *Columbia* had dining rooms, staterooms for those wise enough to make reservations over six months in advance, and ample floor space for sleeping bags, both inside and out. We boarded just late enough to miss grabbing a spot outside on the deck that was protected from the rain. The covered area was strewn with sleeping bags, spots already claimed. Reaching for cover, we snuggled right up beside Chava and her husband as the rains descended on us.

The shoreline changed gradually over the three days of the trip as we left behind the more populated shores of Washington State. We passed infrequent communities along the British Columbia coastline and stopped in the Southeast Alaskan communities of Ketchikan, Wrangell, and Petersburg before arriving in downtown Juneau early in the morning. We pulled into a dock that was right at the foot of a towering mountain. Mt. Roberts, alongside Mt. Juneau, towered more than 3,000 feet—right over the small, colorful downtown section of Juneau that lined the waterfront.

While Loren rested in a hotel room to catch up on needed sleep, I was far too excited to stay put. I had never considered myself someone looking for a place to call home, but I knew from the moment we arrived that I'd found it anyway. I passed by a small apartment with a For Rent sign on the door, knocked, looked around its few square feet, and took it. I didn't check things thoroughly and ended up renting a place where the hot water didn't work. As compensation, the owners offered the steam bath in their rustic hotel a few blocks away.

Waking from his nap to find we had an apartment, Loren concluded I was serious about this job in Juneau. He decided to take the ferry home to collect our belongings. His ferry passed though the smaller community of Sitka, where he disembarked just long enough to call the local tugboat outfit and asked if they had any work in the area. They did. Was there any chance he could get to Seattle, where a tug awaited a deckhand before heading north? One of those romantic tugs we had watched. Our move to Alaska was finalized.

We found our own tugboat two years later. Although she had plenty of rotten wood, she was gorgeous to look at, probably more from a distance than up close. She had beautiful lines, just as we'd dreamed. The *Madrona* had a small wheelhouse with one bunk, a large, beautiful wheel for steering, and an old brass compass. The wheelhouse was our guestroom and was often full. Aft and separate was the compact galley, with a table and benches that could squeeze in four. In yet another small compartment was the head, just a simple toilet with seawater flush. To get to our sleeping quarters, we had to enter through yet another door, climb down a ladder into the engine room, and then walk around the huge Caterpillar engine and forward into an area designed to sleep four. We built a large bunk in the forward fo'c'sle, which provided ample room for sleeping as well as a place to host a group of guitar players and singers. There were more bunks between the fo'c'sle and the engine room, which we used for clothes, tools, and storage. Despite the rot, she was a fine little working tug and a delightful home for years.

Loren found our charming fifty-five-foot tug at a U.S. Marshal's sale, an auction. He bought this first home of ours for a thousand dollars. While working on one of the tugs for his job, he called me periodically to see if the sale papers had arrived. "They're here," I was finally able to say after an envelope from the U.S. Coast Guard had arrived. I hadn't opened it, but I was happy to hear him so excited. I didn't realize he was near Wrangell where the *Madrona* was waiting for us. Nor did I understand he planned to talk the skipper of the tugboat he was working on into letting him bring it home alongside the logs they had in tow. It was headed for Sitka, where I had moved to join Loren.

Within the week, the tug he worked aboard was back in town, along with our "new" old tug. With the envelope still unopened at home, I joined him after work at the tidal grid, a structure of large, parallel wooden beams about four or five feet apart that a boat can run up on at high tide. As the tide recedes, a boat already tied to the dock is high and dry and sits on the beams. This allows for an opportunity to inspect the bottom of the vessel and do some work on it, at least until the tide comes back in. We were both excited and ready to get to work on it.

Within moments, the police arrived to charge Loren with piracy. We didn't own the boat yet. He had taken the boat before it was ours. We didn't have the right papers.

2. OFFERING—*Now*

Tea with God and Drie. That's what I call my morning ritual. It's been twenty-three years since we moved north on the ferry. We stayed in Sitka for about thirteen of those years, moved south for two years, and then moved back to Juneau, a dynamic community of somewhere around 30,000 people. Of my morning companions, God is difficult to describe. For the most part, the name or word—God—seems to point me toward a way I want to see, to walk, to be. Drie, on the other hand, is more tangible. She's a cat. She and I get up before my husband, Loren. She's nine years old, has long, gray hair, and is one of those cats that move about with an air of royalty, no clue she's anything but the queen of the house. Each morning when I rise, from her petite and dignified pose, I am lectured angrily, without ceasing, an insistent, monotonous, and boisterous rant. This goes on until I make my morning tea and finally sit with her in my lap. She's immediately content, purring. Her brother doesn't have much to say. He reserves that for our son, AD, when he comes home from college. Our yellow lab simply wags her tail. Finally, with tea in hand and Drie on my lap, we sit, as we do each day, for our time of silence and prayer. Our living room windows are filled with the tall, green forest, and the log walls around us are comforting arms, an easy place to feel held.

I sit quietly for a while, watching my breath, sipping tea, and listening to the noise of my mind, the quiet of our home, and the wind whistling through the trees. I love the forest around us. It wraps me in a timeless peace, whether soft and silent or wild with storm. I rest in a peace-of-God place, and when I finish, I pick up a small book about women saints and mystics. I've been studying these women with close friends. I read about Anna, the elderly Jewish seer who prophesized about Jesus at the Temple of Jerusalem. She became a saint in the Roman Catholic and Eastern Orthodox Churches. I read about her life of fasting and prayer, her recognition of Jesus as the Christ. How did she see? What was it she saw? I call upon her wisdom for guidance in my life as I offer, "I am ready," I pause and surprise myself as I finish, "for whatever you have in mind for me." I am awed at the sound of conviction and the open-ended offer I have just made. I'm pretty sure the offer is to God, not Anna. In the back of my mind, I'm imagining a new job after ten years of working with hospice, but I don't make that clear.

By the evening, I am in the emergency room with one of Juneau's surgeons, a big, burly fellow who looks like he walked out of the wilderness of rural Alaska. He pulls out a huge knitting needle and thrusts it into my chest. I felt perfectly well this morning, and now there is a huge needle in my chest. Is this a play or a story about someone else? Something we could back up and undo? What about that offer I made this morning? I said I was ready for anything, but I didn't mean this. This feels unreal. The pain, however, is incredibly real.

"Please," I beg, "pain medicine."

I have a collapsed lung, and the knitting needle makes a hole in my chest where the doctor can insert a flexible tube. Normally, a vacuum space or air lock between each lung and the tissue surrounding it function to keep the lung expanded, enabling me to breathe. Somehow, my vacuum was invaded, and my lung has fallen down, collapsed like a deflated balloon. Outside air has collected in the lung space and needs to get out. A collapse, or pneumothorax, is usually caused by a stabbing, a gunshot wound, or an accident. It can become a life-threatening emergency when the air buildup inside the chest becomes great enough to interfere with blood return to the heart.

"Want this as a souvenir?" the doctor jokes, holding up the gooey knitting needle.

As the tube goes in, air rushes out, allowing my lung to re-inflate. Since I don't have a wound caused by stabbing, gunshot, or accident, we all start wondering how such a thing could have happened.

"Maybe too much sex?" offers the ER nurse. We all chuckle.

My friend Mary has come to join the group, and she's certain this has been caused by my running. We've worked together with the local hospice agency, sharing the work of caring for patients day after day, year after year. We've grown close enough to tell each other what to do and what not to do. She's been after me about my running. "I've been telling you, it's not good for you." Tall, slender, athletic men experience a lung collapse on occasion. I'm not tall, not male. Are slender and athletic enough?

I have been running, trying to increase my speed. Having run for years, I'm consistently the slowest runner I've ever met. Another hospice nurse and dear friend, Kathy, laughed with me as I came in last out of hundreds of runners in the Juneau breast cancer support run. "I thought you ran," she said.

"Yes," I responded, breathless. "I've just always been slow." I've always believed others simply run too fast. Aren't you supposed to work out only to the point where you can still talk? Still, I'm working this summer to step it up because I plan to run on a Klondike team.

The Klondike Trail of '98 International Road Relay offers, as its race guide states, "breathtaking scenery, team camaraderie, physical challenge, gracious northern hospitality." The race will begin in Skagway, Alaska, and follow the Gold Rush Stampeder's trail through British Columbia and into Whitehorse, Yukon Territory. I really want to do this with my son, my friends, and their kids. We won't be one of the serious teams. Strictly for fun. We hope for clear skies, Northern Lights, and no snow.

We will party and dance with people from all over the world when we finish. I love that this race is open, as the guide says, to "everyone and anyone." I qualify. Each team will have ten members, handing off to one another throughout the night, covering 176.5 kilometers, a little over a hundred miles.

After work today, I met up with another friend, another Mary, to run together. She's fast, and I'm hoping running with her will help me increase my speed. I ran with AD when he was home recently. He's been patient and kind to run with me. He's really fast and, like Mary, has a vested interest, being on my Klondike team. I ran agonizingly faster than usual today, barely noticing the forested trail alongside the Mendenhall River in Juneau. I love Mary; we always have so much to talk about; I needed her to cover all the talking while we ran fast. I'm grateful she can tell a good tale, because for five miles I could not utter one word. Afterward, I drove downtown to meet Loren, and suddenly, walking up stairs, I was barely able to catch my breath.

I stay in the hospital a few days to give the hole in my lung a chance to seal up. The general consensus is that the collapse was due to my athletic nature and is a once-in-a-lifetime event.

We head home, a long way "out the road." I sit once again, surrounded by these warm log arms of our home, with the cats, the dog, Loren, and my sister Mary, who has come over from Sitka to offer support. I am so glad to be home, breathing, with the nightmare behind us. I take a sip of wine, a bite of dinner, and sneeze. Suddenly, I can barely get my breath, all over again.

"No way," Mary says as we rush to the emergency room. "You're kidding!" But I'm not.

3. SOFT SCRUB—*Then*

My sister Mary joined us in Alaska shortly after we moved there. We were not particularly close as children. I screeched at my younger siblings if they didn't perform their parts correctly in my plays. And Mary, five years younger, not only competed with me for our middle sister's attention, but was noisy in seeking attention so that she wouldn't be left out by the older kids. We left her out.

A few years earlier, she joined us in Seattle where she and Loren worked building boats and I attended nursing school. While driving a long-distance truck between Washington and California, Loren had stopped to visit Mary and listened to her complain about not liking college. "Then why go?" She couldn't think of a single answer and left soon after to join us in Seattle, to my mother's dismay.

So, it was no surprise she then joined us in Alaska, always up for an adventure. In my mind, she was still a lot younger. She'd been picking flowers on a mountainside in Hawaii and was dedicated to living a pure life in bare feet. The cold, unforgiving rain and winds she found in Alaska were strong enough to get her into rubber boots. And I convinced her to make an exception from living the pure life: Juneau's Red Dog Saloon.

Loren was busy with the tugboat job in Sitka, and he and I visited one another, ferrying on the "blue canoes" back and forth between Sitka and Juneau for a few months. Just as with Juneau, there were no roads into Sitka. Boats and planes were the means of accessing many of Southeast Alaska's communities. Eventually, I left my nightshift job at the hospital in Juneau, and Mary and I boarded a ferry to Sitka. We arrived in the small community facing the Pacific Ocean, home to the Tlingit people, its original inhabitants, along with many others who were drawn by the fishing, logging, and beauty.

The small community of approximately 8,000 residents was the first capital of Alaska, sold by the Russians to the United States in 1867. "Seward's Folly" was the term used to describe the 7.2 million dollar sale, referring to Secretary of State William H. Seward. The Russians had arrived and assumed ownership despite the fact that people already inhabited the land. And the Americans bought it as if it was the Russian's property to sell.

Mary and I walked back and forth on Katlian Street, which lined the waterfront. Rows of fishing vessels in the harbors, new, old, large, and small, filled the harbor. We walked by the cannery, where fish was sold and prepared for market, the Native Hall, assorted low-key storefronts, and the Pioneer Bar, busy enough even mid-day. We hoped to find Loren and the tug he worked on but were not successful. This was well before cell phones. We gave up and continued walking about and enjoying the nice day.

Early in the afternoon, a man stepped from a dusty storefront and said, "Maybe I can be of some help. You girls sure do look like you're looking for someone or something. You've walked by here a number of times."

Sheepishly, I explained, "We just moved here, and I have a husband working on a tugboat that doesn't appear to be here. We kind of have to figure out a place to stay." Our only plan had been to look for Loren.

That evening, we toasted to our good fortune in Thompson Harbor, one of Sitka's three boat harbors. The considerate fellow on Katlian Street had referred us to some boat owners who might appreciate having someone living aboard their vessels and keeping an eye on them. Our new city of fishing vessels. Water lapped against the sides of our homes, we heard the distant sounds of a few cars, and the music from another vessel felt welcoming and warmed our souls. Eagles soared overhead. There were plenty of noisy seagulls, and by nightfall a sky full of stars. Our homes smelled musty, and soon we did, too.

Both boats were about thirty-five feet long. The one Mary was on had a unique style and a nasty leak but was still cute and charming. My new home looked a lot like many of the other fishing boats in the harbor—ready for work, with fish hooks and lures lining the interior walls. Both boats had small diesel stoves, which we used for cooking and warmth.

We grew exhausted each day from breaking crab knuckles at cannery jobs, and it felt good. For months, I had worked the nightshift in Juneau's busy hospital that hired me as a new-graduate nurse. I came cheap, but my inexperience loaded up the other nurses with more work than the already-large-enough load they had. Breaking crab was a welcome change. Afterward, we would walk home to the harbor, heading to our boats to start up the stoves. We met for dinner at one or the other's boat, and when Loren returned from one of his two-week trips, he joined us. He would stay with me overnight, unless the inside of my home was lined with ice from winter's chill. Those nights, he returned to his warm tugboat bunk.

The rains of Southeast Alaska are too much for many newcomers to bear. I understand. Growing up in California, a rainy day was referred to as "a bad day." It rained continuously for days in our new rainforest home. We grew strong arms over the next few months as we bailed Mary's boat with a bucket night after night. It was a fine trade, bailing for homes. Clad in rubber boots that we removed only to sleep and warm coats we never changed, we would brush our teeth together at the dock's water spigot, in rain or snow.

"Can you believe we could be having such fun?" asked one or the other, with a mouth full of toothpaste. Mary caught up with me in age those years. Or we caught up with each other, sharing wild adventures on the rough seas or in the dark green forest. She was and still is an energetic adventurer, and some of that began to rub off on me. She certainly was no longer my pesky little sister, and I turned out to be kinder than I had been when we were young. Recently, as I began to write these short tales, she was visiting. She poured a glass of red wine and set the bottle on the counter. I hurried to put something under it to keep the wine from staining my countertop.

"Don't worry," Mary said.

In my older-than-you voice, I said, "I'm protecting the countertop."

"You can just use Soft Scrub."

"Soft Scrub?" How did she learn this before I did? I'm the older sister.

4. I HAVE WHAT?—*Now*

The run to the hospital in our old blue van is long and harried. Mary continues to ask if I'm kidding. Breathless, I shake my head in response. We live so far out the road that it's faster to drive me in than call 911. We know that well, because my friend Trish drove out to our home not long ago, was hit by another car on the way, yet walked away, thinking she was fine. She stood up after dinner and collapsed. It took a very long time for the ambulance to arrive. I was left very appreciative of the energy healing I'd been studying.

It isn't doing me any good just now, or then again, maybe it is. I don't feel like I'm getting any air, gasping for what I can, yet I'm still upright.

After the new tube and more pain medicine goes in, I am lying, once again, in the hospital in Juneau where I first took a job twenty-three years ago. My phone rings; a friend, another Kathy, explains that she knows a woman in Juneau who has a strange, horrible disease with cysts of the lungs, cysts that pop, causing lungs to collapse. I wonder why on earth she's telling me this. I couldn't possibly have a horrible disease. I'm too healthy. I do healing work on others. I've taught people all over the state of Alaska about healthy eating, optimal fitness, and managing stress. Not only that, I'm a hospice nurse. I help others; I'm not the one needing help. "Okay," I say, "thanks for calling, Kathy." anxious to get off the subject.

A CT scan reveals I do have the disease. It's called Lymphangioleiomyomatosis, LAM for short. I'm shocked as I look at the scan pictures of my once-beautiful lungs that have taken me up every mountain in Juneau. This is horrible news. It's a progressive disease, gradually enabling cysts to replace all the alveoli of my lungs. Cysts that will blow. It will render me breathless. The alveoli are essential for the air exchange, letting oxygen into the bloodstream and carbon dioxide out. When I check out this disease online, I learn all sorts of terrible news. I have five to ten years to live. I can expect more collapses like the ones I've had, maybe even coughing up blood. I get chills as I recall being upside down in yoga class last winter, feeling liquid collecting in my throat. When I ran to the bathroom, I spit out a fair amount of blood. I had shrugged it off, thinking it was caused by the long back-country ski trip I had done earlier in the week when the weather was well below freezing.

I learn that approximately a thousand people have been diagnosed with this disease, and it only affects women. It is suspected there are far more women with this disease, as many go undiagnosed for years, even by lung specialists. It turns out I'm fortunate, as my doctor has seen this before. I don't have to wait years for the right diagnosis like many of the women who have it. He has seen it in the woman my friend called me about.

I am to be medevac'd south, flown in a small plane with two nurses monitoring my breathing and other vital signs, helping to keep me alive until I get to a larger facility in Seattle. I am stunned by all of this. It's serious!

My parents had flown up from California when I was re-admitted, and as I'm carted off to my small plane, my father hands me a beautiful gardenia bloom. They know I love them. I know from this gift I'll be okay.

As the plane takes off, I can hear the nurses quietly discussing the charger for the suction machine. They don't intend to involve me, but I'm a nurse, and I figure out what they're discussing. It seems the charger for the suction machine to keep my lung inflated was not working last night. The suction machine is needed to keep my lung inflated so that I can breathe. O my God! I think of my sister Mary on our last ride to the emergency room, and I say, "No way. You're kidding." They aren't.

5. YES, I CAN—*Then*

I sat on the bow, focusing intently on the water below, looking for rocks to avoid as Loren piloted our tugboat, with a barge in tow, slowly into Windham Bay. Sixty miles south of Juneau, we traveled through a long, narrow entrance of lush Southeast Alaskan forest to reach our destination at the head of the bay. The only sounds we could hear came from our noisy Caterpillar diesel engine, with its screaming turbocharger. When we reached the end of our journey, we slowed to pull the barge alongside, snuggled up to it, tied it securely to the tug, and set the anchor. After that, with the engine off, we set about enjoying the tranquility and grandeur surrounding us.

Toasting our good fortune to have found this handsome, only partially rotten tug along with occasional work for her to do in stunningly gorgeous settings, we relaxed for the evening. As the tide came in the next morning, we beached the barge near the place where a lodge was to be built and proceeded to spend the day offloading a large load of lumber. The receding tide left us ample time to get it all off. We planned to float the barge again at high tide.

The tide crept in slowly but surely, and when it did, our barge did not float as we expected. Instead, due to the steep angle of the beach, the water crept into an opening on her deck. Loren moved into action in his usual swift manner. He had our bilge pump working to reverse the water flow. It wasn't enough; we needed a larger pump. He tried to make radio calls so he could order to have one sent out. To no avail. Windham Bay extended a long way from the normally traveled water routes, and mountains blocked any signal. Our magical retreat into wonderland came at a cost: no contact.

I watched as Loren motored off in our tugboat. How I loved the lines of that black hull, the cute wheelhouse, and main deck cabin, with new blue and white paint. That screaming turbocharger wasn't my favorite part of the boat, and it grew faint as Loren headed back out of the bay, leaving me ashore with the barge, bilge pump, a bucket, and our skiff. I looked hopelessly at the scene before me, wondering how far back out the bay he would have to go before he could call for a pump to be sent out.

I watched our barge fill with water, thinking, it's a damn good thing I keep my winter job nursing. Our learning curve was quite often steep enough to end up costing us instead of lining our pockets. Suddenly, it hit me: maybe I could work faster than the little bilge pump. "I'll give it a try," I announced to the barge and the bay. I climbed down the hatch inside the barge and began offloading water: bucket by bucket.

I kept at it for about four hours. In all honesty, I loved it; I loved working as hard as I possibly could. There was something about sweating in paradise that captured my spirit. I didn't stop for a moment. By early afternoon, when the sun was obscured by the tall trees that abutted the water's edge of sand and rock, the "no-see-ums" started in on me. I knew I shouldn't stop, not even long enough to swat at the damn bugs. Loren had been gone hours, and I heard nothing coming—not him and the tug, nor any plane delivering a pump.

By late afternoon, I had the barge afloat. I was elated. I'd done it. I let out a little line from the skiff tied to the barge and climbed in. I started up the engine and headed into the center of the bay, away from the beach, slowly towing my accomplishment behind me. Just as I did, I could see the *Madrona* heading toward the head of the bay. No sooner had I spotted her than a float plane dropped in as well, delivering a pump.

My face and arms were covered with hundreds of bites and itched like hell for a week. And still, I loved it.

6. YES, I DID—*Now*

The nurses on the evacuation flight cannot charge the suction machine and use it to keep my lung inflated at the same time. They alternate, charging awhile and then hooking it up to my tube for a while. We're on a tiny jet; the nurses are right beside me, only inches away. Of course I can hear them whispering. The sound of the plane's engine is a welcome hum, I suspect, for all of us. I can see that Loren, folded into his small space on the other side of me, is terrified. I think I'm somewhere beyond terrified. This is all far too unreal, and apparently it's quite real. I know it's dangerous flying with the suction not working. I know it's risky just flying with a hole in my lung. I watch myself, afraid I will die, and I watch myself knowing that there's nothing at all I can do except lie still and smell the gardenia. Inhaling is my prayer. And exhaling. Inhaling again and again, the smell of the flower. Over and over, I pray and breathe my way to Seattle.

Arriving safely, the nurses at constant attention, I'm offloaded to an ambulance, and we weave our way through the streets of Seattle. Once hospitalized, I'm ushered into surgery to have my pleura roughed up. A pleurodesis. The pleura is a thin, two-layered membrane that lines the inside of the chest cavity and covers the lungs. There is a negative pressure between the layers, creating a vacuum that holds up the lungs. Mine won't stay up because the cyst caused a hole in one lung, and that hole allowed air into the vacuum space. My lungs are like a balloon that has popped, and to get it back in working order again, we have to glue it up, hole and all. At this point, roughing up the pleura with an instrument of some kind will cause everything to get irritated and inflamed and stick together—the glue job. It sounds horrible to me, but right now my lung is being held up by another suction machine. My glued-up lung won't be as flexible as it once was, but it should at least stay up, allowing me to breathe. I am warned it may not work.

No one gets to stay long in hospitals anymore. I am sent home a few days after the surgery and am told that the surgery may not hold. My mind is preoccupied with that fact. I am afraid of moving, that I may sneeze, bend over incorrectly. I'm terrified of another breathless collapse. Loren and I lie awake at night, too frightened to sleep.

While I sit, trying to read, mostly dazed, Loren spends time researching this new development in our lives. It appears I am fortunate to be alive. Many women with LAM die much younger. Pregnancy is often difficult, triggering lung collapses. Some of the women who get this disease, once stabilized with lungs that will stay up, do not continue to accumulate more cysts as they age. Others deteriorate rapidly. Again, we face the numbers: five to ten years to live.

In Cincinnati, Ohio, there is a woman named Sue Byrnes. When she learned that her daughter was diagnosed with this eleven-syllable disease, she decided she would do everything she could to put an end to this. She worked tirelessly to set up a foundation that offers support to women and their families who receive this news. The foundation raises funds and lobbies for research money. NIH is studying LAM, bringing women to stay for a week in Bethesda year after year, allowing them to understand the disease process and study possible interventions. Our burden of terror and isolation is lightened as Loren talks with Sue and learns as much as possible.

While our sense of isolation is lightened, my breathing feels worse. It seems that it's harder to breathe each hour. Am I making this up? Is my terror causing my breathlessness? The doctor said it was fine when I was discharged. Is he right—that it's fine? Or is my lung falling down again? I can't stand this. I can't escape. I'm exhausted and terrified.

My breathing has gotten so bad that I can't deny the gasping now. There's no position I can get in to improve my chances of getting enough air.

We head back to the hospital. The roughing-up has not held the lung up. Once again, a tube goes in my chest, and I'm hooked up to suction. Will this never end? Will my lung never stay up, and will the hole never heal? A group of doctors enter my room after having thoroughly reviewed my records and studied the CT scan of my lungs. "It says in your note here that you frequently hiked and cross-country skied during the past year, sometimes up to thirteen miles in a day. That isn't possible, given the picture we have of your lungs. Is this what you meant to say or have you been exaggerating?"

"No," I reply, "I've been doing that for years—one large peak hiked just days before the collapse."

They smile and look knowingly at one another as one comments, "That's very unlikely."

7. RIDING A WAVE—*Then*

A large wave stacked up in front of us, and before we could turn, we were headed into it. I don't know the words anyone else uttered, but I recall a torrent of both prayers and cussing coming from me. The tug headed straight up, as if headed to heaven. Plates and mugs and pots and pans were flying as I wedged myself in place, staring out the window, watching the world turn on its side. We rode straight up and up—and then straight down. As we dove, the small refrigerator flew open, its contents flying out before me, and then the unit itself crashed into the tiny space of our galley.

***

I had indeed married a "boat-guy," one of those people happiest on and around boats. I had my hands full with plenty to learn, as I had been the kind of person who loved to watch boats from the shore. Admire their lines, dream of sailing off into the sunset. I loved work as a nurse, whether assisting in the delivery of babies, traveling to small communities, or working with Alaska's elderly at the Sitka Pioneer Home. It was a good thing because our boat work didn't start providing us with much to live on for some years. One breakdown left us needing a thousand dollars for a new screaming turbocharger for the engine. I hired out for a few weeks with a family to care for an elderly parent while the rest of the family went on vacation. I made enough to afford us a new turbocharger.

When asked these days about when he plans to retire, Loren says, "Oh, I retired in my twenties." I kept nursing each winter.

I can't say that I ever fully embraced being a mariner. When Sitka was threatened with a tsunami, all the boats except two left the harbor to ride it out, the owners preferring to ride over the wave than to have their boats dumped on top of the Pioneer Bar. The two that remained were under my care. Loren was out of town, and so was my brother-in-law, Kerry. I was responsible for both boats. I paced the near-empty dock, looking nervously at our boats. I could tow Kerry's boat behind ours if I had to. I debated a good long ten minutes before heading for high ground, letting the boats ride out the tsunami on their own. I didn't want to take four-year old AD out there to ride over the wave and I didn't want to leave him behind. That big wave never did materialize, and I was deeply relieved.

There was always something new for me to learn. Like taking the wheel in six-foot ocean swells because our tow came loose and Loren had to go retrieve it. Or figuring out how to get a large male sea lion to stop taking bites at our towline, a line with two Forest Service house boats tied to the other end of it. Often as not, it concerned the head. Easy to plug, yucky to fix, disastrous when broken, it's no wonder heads fill plenty of my memory cells. In the days before boats were outfitted with holding tanks for sewage, everything went straight into the water, including the beeper I carried as an obstetric nurse on-call at the hospital. It slipped right out of my back pocket as I finished using the head, and I watched in shock as it sank below the water's surface. A jammed head brought me to near hysteria when I was pregnant, and I cried, jumped ship, and flew off, leaving Loren to finish the job with another deckhand.

Our temperamental head blew up on my sister Mary. Fortunately, the surroundings in Glacier Bay National Park included calving glaciers, seal pups on icebergs, and a vast expanse of land and water newly uncovered by retreating glaciers, softened the impact. So did our great hot shower. Earlier in the day, we had grabbed ahold of a large iceberg with a couple of ropes and then hauled it onto the back deck with our hydraulic crane. It was about six feet in diameter and took well over a week to melt. We chipped off ice to add to a glass of whiskey, and I had it ready for her as she emerged from her hot shower.

It wasn't a temperamental head that got us in trouble when we encountered the steep wave that took us up and slammed us back down. We did a lot of odd jobs with our old tug, often towing others who were setting out to seek fortune and adventure. The big wave found us when we were moving friends to Elfin Cove, a small community on the northwestern coast of Chichagof Island, a 2,000 square-mile island, referred to by many as "God's country." Chichagof Island is just north of Baranof Island, on which Sitka is located. Traveling the direct route would have taken us only one day, but through the rough waters of the outside coast. Instead, preferring a gentler trip, we took a longer route, leisurely traveling inside waters, a four-day trip. Our friends were moving to this small fishing community consisting of a store, lodge-in-progress, fuel dock, and a handful of homes that lined the quiet boardwalk in the secluded cove.

Shortly before reaching our destination, we traveled through South Inian Pass with their small boat in tow. Any old salt worth their rubber boots could tell you when not to pass through South Inian Pass. We were just new and young enough to be not particularly salty. We had not made the adjustment from the tide book data for daylight savings time. We headed into the pass, where a large body of water moves during the tidal change from ebb to flood or vice versa. We thought we were going to hit slack current—the time when the tidal current is changing from one direction to the other, therefore slack. But we were an hour late, and once in, it was too late to turn back. And on top of that there was a west wind blowing, which made the resulting wave the current created, stack up even higher.

Straight up and straight down. Every room of the vessel was strewn with things that had escaped from their careful placement. Even things fairly well secured had at least shifted. Their little boat in tow behind us was drenched but afloat.

Like all the supplies in their little boat, we got a lot saltier that day.

8. RIDING ANOTHER KIND OF WAVE—*Now*

I look out the window from my hospital bed. It's fall. Orange, brown, and red leaves are being lifted right off of branches as the season's wind sails through the boughs. Fall is my favorite season. It's as if a burden lifts each year when fall returns. It is the time of year I can rest. The intensity of summer's activity lightens. The wind is a sister, easy and familiar to walk with. She makes the leaves dance and my heart swell.

I am livid. I want to be out there! I want to dance with the fall leaves, to walk, skip, and run back home in Juneau. We are still south, unable to return to Juneau because my lung won't stay up. My hospital bed is beside the wall once again, where the suction machine sits. Since the surgery to glue up my lung, this is the second time I have been admitted, needing a chest tube and the machine to suck my lung back up. Each run to the hospital has been terrifying. Having been hooked up to suction for one day, I am now unhooked, and we are hoping I can continue breathing without the machine, that the surgery worked after all. And that they will send me home again.

I stare at the suction machine, turned off, but ready to resume its sucking noise once again if I run out of breath. If that happens, I'm to call the nurse, and the machine will be hooked up to my tube, and once again, I'll be tethered to it so that I can breathe. How on earth did I get hooked up with this scene? Just about three weeks ago, I was biking to work, spending hours each day talking in a booming voice to hundreds of tourists, enjoying their excitement watching humpback whales, sea lions, harbor seals, and more. Then spending a few hours cleaning the boat, riding home, going for a run. The leaves had barely turned. I was taking a break from working with hospice patients and enjoying my time working aboard tour boats.

Now I'm trapped here, with a terminal disease. It looks as if I'll be the hospice patient. Damn! When I was admitted two days ago to the Emergency Room, a doctor thrust another tube into my chest and then had to leave for another emergency. The tube was up against my spine and the pain unbelievably severe. I moaned and begged for the nurses to move it, to pull it out, just a little. It was sewn in; they could not. They drugged me senseless instead.

My small, aging mother struggled to help me remove my tall boots. "Why won't they come off?" I moaned.

"Why on earth do I wear shoes that won't come off?" I was in so much pain and so drugged—in a fruitless attempt to alleviate that pain—that my mind was enveloped in fog and I couldn't help her. I couldn't cry; it hurt too much. My mother wept for me.

She is with me again in this room with the waiting suction machine. It is such a comfort to have her with me. I'm brokenhearted that my pain brought her to tears, but I can't undo it. We're backwards here. I said I'd take care of my folks; I'm the family nurse. How did things get reversed?

My roughed-up lung falls down again. I can tell; I am gasping. I feel as though I cannot get any air. At least I'm in a hospital and won't have to rush to an ER. We ring for help. No one can reach the doctor to order the suction machine to be hooked back up to my chest tube. How can it take so long to get an order? My gasping is audible. I'm straining and desperate. I watch helplessly as my mother suffers, again, watching me struggle.

The doctor is found an hour into this scene and orders an X-ray to prove I can't breathe and that it's caused by a collapsed lung. A kind nurse apologizes for how long it's taking just to get an X-ray tech. I can do nothing but open my mouth wide and continue my noisy gasping. Once the busy doctor is shown the X-ray, I am re-attached to the machine. Geez, I am such a wimp! Why didn't I just disobey the nurse and hook myself back up? Without an X-ray or doctor. Honestly!

After two days of being hooked up and then cut loose from suction again, I feel as though it's coming around to hook-up time again. When I lean forward, air gurgles up as I stand. I am mildly panicking, but at least I'm in a hospital. "It's leaking! The vacuum isn't working," I tell the doctor.

My mouth drops as he responds, "It's time to leave the hospital." He's done all he can, and the pleurodesis, the glue job, should work.

"Please," I beg. "I know my lung isn't up yet."

"You can't know that, and you have a terminal illness, and you'll have to get used to it." Oh my God.

It's the same thing all over again as I head to a relative's home in the area. I'm watching every breath, terrified to sleep, afraid that my lungs will fall and I'll be gone. I walk carefully, don't bend over, don't reach high, and don't lift. I'm a porcelain doll. Loren and I lie in bed; he touches me so gently, afraid to break me.

Over and over, "Am I breathing as well as an hour ago, as yesterday?" I ask Loren. I don't know what to do, and he doesn't either. I do think it's getting worse each day.

Like a broken record, I'm back in and hooked up again in a few days. This time, I've tried another hospital. I kept putting off coming in, so I'm horribly short of breath by the time I get here. I wanted the glue job to work. The doctor said it would work. I was so terrified. This time, I have a lot of tubes. The roughed-up lung is glued up all over and fallen down all over, so all the tubes are placed in strategic places with some kind of X-ray or CT scan. If a tube gets put in where the lung is stuck, there could be a new and lethal hole to deal with. A new pleurodesis is tried; my lung is glued up with talc. Talc, yes, like the baby powder. It's an irritant, more aggressive than the roughing-up job. And when I go home, the tube is left hanging from my chest wall so that if my lung collapses again, I can rush to an ER and be hooked up, once again, to suction. Loren has a large needle he can stick into a designated place in my upper chest if we can't get to help. Need to get that air out somehow. He keeps it out of my sight.

I am tentatively elated to be breathing and able to walk tenderly, gingerly, among the few remaining leaves. We stay in the home of another friend, near the hospital. Family and friends have been at our side, offering prayers and support, this entire time. Our hearts are heavy with trepidation and fear on one hand and with awe and gratitude on the other. We have been surrounded by love.

After a few weeks pass, we move in with my parents, who are the kindest people I know. My brothers, sisters, and friends have traveled from their homes, and I can't imagine dealing with all of this without them. When I wake in the hospital to wonder who I am and where on earth I am, compliments of pain medications, someone has been there to guide me home to earth, to reach the nurse when I need to pee and the buzzer is out of reach, or to sit beside me all night in an uncomfortable chair so I won't be alone or run out of breath again.

Loren manages a fleet of boats in Juneau for a company based in Sitka. He's been with me two months already. They have loaned us the car they keep in Seattle this entire time. We are overwhelmed by kindness, filled with gratitude.

Each day I can still breathe, fear recedes bit by bit. Has it simply moved back out to sea where another tidal wave awaits? The terror I feel is softened, its edges turned mushy by all the love and care. The more we learn from the LAM Foundation, the less frightened we feel, despite the dismal future.

Now I can watch Loren. He's been staying connected to his work throughout this period, carrying his work load by phone and carrying his worry about me as well. He is moving through all this as if his body wore the bruising. Not only must he manage getting me to doctors and hospitals, figuring out where we'll stay, but he actually feels the chest pains and breathlessness. Moving through each day and trying to sleep at night, his terror is mingled with mine. We are both afflicted with this terminal thing.

Finally, three months after flying south with gardenia prayers, we are ready to travel home to Juneau. We don't fly to Alaska because it's thought that the cysts in my lungs cause holes that can pop, which would leave me breathless in the sky. So we board the ferry and spend three days and nights, traveling from Bellingham, Washington to Juneau. I'm still asking, "Is this really happening? Do I have an illness that will render me unable to breathe in five to ten years?" I look in the mirror on the ferry and see the dark circles under my eyes, and with every movement, I feel the block of cement in my chest. That's the glue job. "Yes," I tell the mirror, "it would seem it is happening."

I rest to the rolling motion of the sea and wake to look out the window of our small stateroom. As I do, tears start streaming; my heart is flooded with joy, and even some calm rushes in like a different tidal wave. I am looking at the wet Southeast Alaskan coast, the tall trees, the dark forest, and the wild waters lapping the rugged and rocky shoreline. I remember how this land speaks to me, how my soul comes out to hear its whispers and roars. This has become my home where the mountains pour into the sea, their steep hillsides often shrouded by misty clouds. I know these woods, these inland waters. I love them, their wildness, the intimacy of the land and sea, the gusting winds, and constant rain.

Despite the skeleton frame I see in the mirror and the echo of my doctor recommending I would be safer to stay south, I look outside the ferry window and know I will be safe here. I got to come home alive, and this wild land will nourish me back to health. Every cell in my body knows.

9. WILD LAND—*Then*

Just after our adventure with the steep wave in South Inian Pass, our son was born. By the time he was nine years old, we had moved from Sitka back to Juneau. Adrian, or AD, as he prefers to be called, was as excited to spend time exploring Juneau's mountains as I was.

On this particular day, AD, the dog, and I were wet from our vigorous hike and muddy from the worn, wet trail. We reached the small grove of trees where I always grew quiet, where a wave of awe settled over me. Really, the awe would envelope me as I entered the forest, but at this spot, it grew deeper. We had wound our way up the mountain, through the forest of spruce and hemlock, blue berries and huckleberries, moss and more moss. Our heads were bowed, our eyes focused on our steps to avoid the roots, rocks, and mud where possible. I loved to stop here. The trees were small, stunted, and an abundance of light filtered through them, in sharp contrast to the dense forest we had walked through. We could lift our eyes to hike at this point, just before we reached the tree line. Off to my left, one of the small trees had spent half its life reaching toward heaven, to the height of my waist, then taken a sharp turn, traveling for a few feet horizontally before once again reaching for the sky. It offered a perfect seat for nine-year-old AD. I felt such exquisite pleasure each time I reached this point of the hike up Mt. Roberts, this chunk of precious earth where the darkness opened up to light. While AD sat on the bend in the tree, our dog rested, and I leaned against another tree to cherish the moment, grateful to be in such company and on this marvelous mountain.

I came to love the mountains and backcountry surrounding the community of Juneau. I spent many of my days off in the woods, atop the tall peaks, along shores or rivers. I found a marvelous group of people to share these trips with, old and young. Each new hike thrilled me, as did returning again and again. Half the year, the trails were covered with snow and ice, and I was challenged to learn to make my way, with cross-country skis on, as deeply into the wild land as I had when the ground was bare. Juneau is cut off from the mainland by the Juneau Icefield, approximately 1,500 square miles of solid ice, in some places over 4,000 feet deep. The ice field is the source of Juneau's glaciers, with cold rivers that flow from them. When adequately frozen, those rivers offer easy access into the backcountry for hikers and skiers.

AD was eager to head to the top on this particular summer day. April, our dog, was eager to go wherever

AD went. Moving upward, we could see a bear walking across the remaining ice in the valley below. Down the other side, far below, the city of Juneau sat at the base of the mountain, stretched out along the shore. Float planes coming and going in the channel took off between mountain peaks. They were small toys from here, the immense cruise ships bathtub boats. Up and up we went. A panorama of majestic mountains encircled us. Dark blue waterways broke up the land masses, some visible, others we knew because we had traveled on them.

Finally at the top, I rested against a rock, looking down the valleys, out beyond one peak after the other as the wind cooled my face while my son and our dog continued exploring the rocky ridge.

AD, the dog, and I explored so many mountain trails in Juneau, just as we traveled the waterways around Sitka with Loren. The country saturated me with awe. I started taking AD into the woods when he was still in a backpack. By four or five years of age, he loved to lure me off the trails. "Come see this, Mom." By ten years old, he was constantly coaxing me along. "Just a little further, Mom. You can do it." His interests evolved beyond mine, into camping trips on the Mendenhall Glacier in Juneau and to climbing the frozen waterfall beside the glacier. "You can do it, Mom" wouldn't work on me then.

I suppose that's not entirely true. Years later, with the oxygen tank on my back and its meter turned up as high as possible, he did coax me up a small climb on the glacier. And I recall a trip he made home from college when he wanted me to find a backpack carrier that could hold an adult—me. He knew how much I missed the backcountry with my limited lung capacity. He intended to hoist me onto his back and haul me up the trail that wound its way between Mt. Juneau and Mt. Roberts and into a basin. We had both fallen in love with that outdoor cathedral, Granite Basin. Certainly, he was strong enough, but I never did find a backpack. We found a backcountry wheelchair, but we couldn't get far, stopped by rocks that had to be climbed over.

Seeing a bear far down the valley on Mt. Roberts was one thing, but up close wasn't a welcome moment. Well before I had breathing trouble, we took a five day backpack trip over the popular Chilkoot Trail, an outdoor museum that follows the gold rush trail of the 1890s through both Alaska and Canada. We both had on new boots—good boots, but new. As we set out, he kept stopping to mess with his boots. I grew impatient with stopping, and deciding he was a much stronger hiker at fourteen years of age and could easily catch up with me, I went on ahead while he did some serious adjusting with his boots. I walked, walked, and walked some more. "My goodness, he's taking an awfully long time with those darn boots," I said to the forest.

Eventually, I turned around. Where on earth is he? "AD! AD!" I shouted, walking back on the trail. It wasn't long before I heard what sounded like a loud cat's meow. Picking up my pace, the meow became clearer.

It was my son's voice: "Mom, bring the bear spray! Mom, bring the bear spray!"

Oh my God. I ran toward him, unstrapping my thirty-pound pack in what seemed like endless places. Eventually free of the pack, grabbing only the bear spray, I ran as fast as possible, yelling, "I'm coming! I'm coming!" As I ran into the clearing, the bear ran off. It had stopped AD on the trail, standing up on its hind legs, sniffing this two-legged son of mine, and then dropping back on all fours and proceeding to walk in circles around AD. Knowing all the right things to do, he had raised his arms to look bigger, made noise, and didn't turn away or run—just backed up slowly. He told me he'd reached around to the side of his pack to grab the bear spray and then remembered it was the water bottle he had. I had the bear spray.

I loved raising my son in such exquisite country. I think the wildness inspired a sense of awe and freedom, a confidence in one's place in the natural world. AD and I were great companions in our love of the backcountry. As he grew more adventuresome, exploring on his own, I considered worrying about him, out alone, but rarely did. We were both respectful of the country we had come to love, and we each prepared with gear and planning. We shared a sense that the wild country was safe, was home.

When we met up with Loren after this trip, AD and I had an agreement not to tell him about the bear encounter. He didn't think much of our ventures into the woods, so we figured everyone would be happiest without telling this particular story. We got into the car, drove off, and within minutes, he asked, "Okay, you two, what are you not telling me?"

10. I WANT MY LIFE BACK—*Now*

We are nestled back into our home, the log walls around us again like warm, strong arms. So many friends calling to offer help, meals, support, anything. At a healing Mass, hundreds of hands rest on my head. Though I am weak and scrawny, I am humbled and blessed.

With all this light around us, Loren and I move about some days in a daze, aware our lives are changed forever. Each breath is important, each person precious, our lives amazing, each new day a gift. It is almost a kind of bliss we share, our eyes opened newly, differently.

And yet, I miss myself, my old self. I wasn't looking for this new and precious sense of life. I loved living as it was. My offer to God and the Universe and St. Anna was for a different job, a move downtown. "I am ready ... for whatever you have in mind for me." Something besides this.

Who am I if I am not running, hiking, biking, taking care of patients, supporting clients in crisis, and meeting life head-on? "How could this happen?" I rage. This was not the plan.

Lots of people have ideas for me. "You should try Reiki."

"What about acupuncture?"

"I have a friend who really likes naturopathy."

"Have you thought about doing some deep grief work? The lungs are associated with grief." Geez! A well-intentioned suggestion, I know. I've heard the lungs are associated with grief before. I've been facilitating grief workshops, for goodness sakes! Enough! Yet here I am in the car, sliding the grief cassette I loan out to others into the player.

"Even though your loved one is gone, he will always be with you," drones a soft voice from my cassette player.

I scream at her: "No, you don't understand, I'm the one going!" The car is my screaming chamber.

I weep as I walk the shore just north of our home, stepping carefully over the rocky ground. It's cold. The rocks are large enough to keep me focused as I walk. I hear eagles overhead. I go back, day after day. The idea of dying is okay, I'm thinking. I've been helping others to do that for the past ten years. But it's the idea of being dependent on someone, Loren or someone else, to help me dress, to use the bathroom, to live gasping. I can't stand this. It won't work! I told my close nurse friends on a hike one day "Give me any disease but a lung disease to die of." And I've said it before. I meant it. Is this some kind of cosmic joke?

There are plenty of folks who have advice, but my close friends say to me as I whine, "I'm sorry." They do not say "Why don't you …?" or "Have you thought about …?" or "It could be worse." They let me hurt. The trees let me pound on them, the rocks and sand just hold me as I collapse into them. The mountains, oh my God, I miss them, still too weak to go deep into the woods. But they wait.

Lymphangioleiomyomatosis. I meet Sally, the other woman, the friend of my friend, who has this disease, too. I look at her, and she doesn't look like me—exhausted, thin, pained, and frightened. "There is life after this, Cathy," she says. She lives a normal life. Yet I live in fear of the cysts in my lungs causing another collapse, the glued lung or the other one. She hasn't had that happen since her first one. She got her life back; that's what I want. I can imagine accepting the idea of dying, but only if I get to work again and to spend my days off deep in the mountains. Who knows—if I can at least strap myself to my cross-country skis, maybe an avalanche will finish me off before this stupid disease does.

***

Days turn to months, and as time passes, I do get stronger. I can get back into the woods, and I feel well enough to return to work. I find a job as an elementary school nurse and have the time of my life. Working as a hospice nurse, I cared for many of the grandparents of these children. As with most of my nursing jobs, I fall in love with the work.

My first year, I'm afraid my lungs will blow and the school will wish they hired someone else. But my lungs stay up. They wait until the summer when school is out, just as my sister Carol and I are heading off on a four-day road trip through the interior of Alaska to see AD graduate from college in Fairbanks. The car is packed, but I feel pain in my back and shortness of breath. An X-ray confirms my lung is down. This is not fair! I'm furious to miss AD's graduation. He's an outstanding student, and I want to cheer him on. I unpack the car, fuming. At least the lung doesn't fall down as terribly as the first time.

With a few weeks of rest, using some oxygen, careful not to lift, strain, or cough, the partial collapse comes back up. Great, enough drama. I am adjusting. I have my life back.

I've resumed my meditation, qigong, and yoga practices. I visualize great health, strong and vibrant lungs. Weekly acupuncture along with Chinese herbs. I mix up the large vat of herbs each week, infusing the house with the aroma. If anyone can stop this from progressing, I can. I'm back on my game. I'm certain I will be one of the women whose lungs don't worsen.

"We should go back to Cincinnati to the LAM conference," Loren offers one evening. He has been researching this breath-robbing disease while I have been trying to ignore the literature, along with any discussion of it.

"Why? I have my life back, I don't want to. I don't want to make this disease who I am. " So he travels to the conference by himself, and when he returns home, he places before me, a graph. He has been graphing the lung function tests I take every three months, worrying about the decline of my lungs. In front of me, I see just when I should be no longer breathing. Honey," I say, "we're going to get ahead of this. I'm not dying then."

Loren tells me what he has learned at the conference about the transplant process, which I attempt to shrug off. He asks me please, please, to get listed. "I'm not asking you to agree to the transplant," he says, "just to get on the list. The wait for people who want lungs is about three years, and half the people waiting die before a lung is found for them."

"Half," I murmur. According to Loren's graph, I'll be gone in four. Dead.

11. PAY MY WAY—*Then*

My beeper went off somewhere after midnight. I had been thinking that this was probably the night my patient—let's call him Ben—would die. I called the hospice answering service and got the phone number to call. "Cathy, he's gone," from Ben's daughter.

"I'll be right there," I offered sadly. I was sad, despite knowing this moment was coming. I dressed quickly and grabbed my hospice bag. It was always ready to go. I headed toward town. The night was clear, the roads pretty much empty. Tall fir and spruce and occasional homes lined the roadside. Death awed and humbled me. Driving in the middle of the night, I had the road to myself with the night sky outlining the trees, and a sense of life's great mystery washed over me as it did often en route to someone's death. I drove by the mountains and bays I had explored and loved, blessed them, and drove on, centering myself. Centering became so important with this job. Whenever I was about to meet a new family, sitting in my car in silence, along the roadside for a few minutes, helped me open to this new family, one of whom was likely to die soon. And en route to a death, I often put in a cassette tape of chants that helped me center, ready myself to witness the pain, grief, and incredible power of the moment.

I arrived at Ben's home, knocked quietly, and entered. Before entering his room, his son whispered, "He really was gone." In his room, there he was, lying awake and alive, in bed.

"Help me up," he said.

I found the work of my life when I began working as a hospice nurse. As hospice nurses, we became like family, helping people to live until they died. Sure, we helped them to die, but it was more. We helped people live out final days as comfortably and meaningfully as possible. The whole family was our patient. We brought to bear the great strides in medicine, not to prolong life, but for palliative care, to provide comfort. This painful moment that we each face can bring out the very best in loved ones, neighbors, and strangers. When a patient has no family, neighbors and church members seem to materialize and become family. I've watched people who are living marginalized lives on the street gather and care for one of their own. It was an honor to work as a hospice nurse, each day holy. The work fit me like a glove. On this particular night, I'd been with the agency six of my ten years. I had fallen in love with this family a few years earlier, when Ben's wife died.

Death invites the memories of other deaths. I escorted those who clung to life and those who left easily. With many of my patients and their families, death was not an acceptable option. I would offer to travel two roads with them; I would support their desire for healing and be happy to be discharged. And I would be available if their process moved them to death. On both paths, my work was to support their living.

My life became enriched. I knew intimately people I may never have met, had I not been their hospice nurse. Characters, everywhere. There was the deaf fellow who boarded the city bus, got off at the University of Alaska, picked most of their blooming tulips, smiled at the folks who came out to try to stop him, exclaiming to them, "They've never been this beautiful!" One night I got a call at home from a patient, an elderly man, calling to make sure I'd read the paper; my son had placed first in a run. And the feisty woman I said goodbye to before I left on a long trip. She was so close to dying, I was sure I wouldn't see her again. She was so angry with me for saying goodbye that she stayed alive just long enough for me to return home, just to prove me wrong. With one family, I skied into the backcountry to spread ashes. Young and old, there were so many tears, so much laughter. As nurses, we loved and were loved.

At a death, once I had determined that a patient had passed, I would wait with the family for the coroner to come for the body. I sat at many kitchen tables, laughing, crying, and reviewing the precious stories shared by family or friends. Tender, that's what it was, always. Tender.

Ben wanted help sitting up. After that, he wanted help moving to sit in his comfortable living room chair. His adult children assisted him there with some difficulty. Once seated, he told them, "I want my checkbook." His son got his checkbook, which Ben placed in his shirt pocket with great care. "I want to pay my way."

And then he died.

12. LEAVING—*Now*

Jerry, one among many adorable kindergarteners, walks in the front door of the school where I work and looks at me, his eyes widening and his jaw dropping. "You already got your lungs?" he asks. Yesterday, the school held a Goodbye, Nurse Cathy assembly where they presented gifts they had made, and I cried as the students learned the reason I was leaving was to have a lung transplant. Yet, here I am still at school the next day. He is amazed, figuring I got them last night.

I will miss these kids and this job even more than the mountains. I have loved being part of the village that raises children. Office staff has been helpful, running to a student who has fallen, using a walkie-talkie to update me and receive my directions as I shuffle to the scene with my oxygen backpack slung over a shoulder. The students who want to see how far we can make my oxygen tank fly if we drop it from the roof won't get their chance.

It turns out I am one of the women in whom the disease does progress. My intense focus on healing, on reversing the decline, isn't working. My ability to breathe is slipping away. Just two days ago, with a freezing temperature outside, I got out of my car, made certain my oxygen was on high, and went up a flight of about twenty-five steps. Halfway, I could not breathe. Even with oxygen, I am far too vulnerable in the cold. Once indoors, I was still gasping for ten minutes and crying for the next ten. I can walk only about a block when I am outside, on flat ground and hooked up to my oxygen on high. It's winter, and the freezing temperatures simply take away my breath. We have installed a device in my car that enables me to start it from indoors so that I can pre-warm it. I finally carry a cell phone.

It can be so frightening. Yet I don't want fear to fill my life, and so I move it aside, trusting as best I can that what breath I need will be there for me. When my breath runs short, fear gets triggered, and I have to stop, slow my breath, take a look at the fear grabbing hold of me, and then watch it go. Watch it move aside. It's as if I go about my life with fear tucked into my pocket. Handy, I suppose, but not particularly enjoyable to pull out so often.

A doctor asked me recently, "How do you live with this, knowing your lungs could collapse again any time?"

All I could come up with as a response was, "How can I not?"

I am surprised to learn that I'm quite vain. I don't like going out wearing my nose-hose. Children stare, adults turn away. I enjoy the children, especially the ones who ask me about it. I remember stats I learned in nursing school: fifty percent of people who need oxygen use it. Many stop going out. I make myself use it; I've never been one to stay put very long. Still, I wrestle with my new image.

The Dalai Lama is on television being interviewed. "If you had one message for the western world, what would it be?"

"That we are vulnerable," he responds immediately. Of course! We are vulnerable, but we live as if we aren't. This helps. I create a new mission: I'll put on my nose-hose and go out, head high, and remind everyone who notices my tube that we're all vulnerable.

That little piece of vulnerability wisdom reaches right inside me, nudging aside feelings of failure—thoughts like, Who am I without all the things that define me? And there's the shame of being sick and having little to contribute anymore. At least for now, this new perspective gives me a credible task: I'll be helpful by spreading "vulnerability awareness."

Tea with God and Drie is changing. I still hope to quiet my mind, but I also want to understand and settle more deeply into the mystery of dying. My dying. I do and I don't want to make this dive. I appreciate the new depths I seem to inhabit, but I honestly think if offered my old life back, I'd leave the depth behind.

I am reaching more deeply into what I understand to be God, renewing the sacraments that filled my younger life. I do this in simple ways. I am baptized each day, wading at the beach or just in the shower, reminded to receive the day, the moment new, reminding myself I am a child of the Divine. My soul is cleansed along with my body. I take communion with my Mary friends. With one Mary, I share wine and hummus. With another, walks through the wetlands, and with yet another, it is creating quilts.

And I do my confessing on the beach where the water can carry it off. I keep dry wood and a sleeping bag in my car. When I want to, I stop at my favorite beach, build a small fire to keep warm, and let the universe know my grief. I confess to the "not-enoughness" that I feel. Not enough without all the things that defined me. I don't want this!

Yesterday, I sat at the water's edge, gazing at the massive, snow-covered peaks of the Chilkat Range across the canal and wept for a long time. "I am afraid. I don't want this. I don't trust life. Please tell me I'll be okay. Please." I lie down, snuggle into the sand, sleeping bag wrapped around me, and fall asleep. I awake to a bird lightly touching down on my chest before it flies off.

I am overwhelmed with gratitude for Loren, for his steady, grounding presence. I think at this point I'd shrivel up and blow away if it weren't for him. As one of his friends jokes, "Hey, Loren, you're raising the bar for the rest of us, buddy."

I asked him to stay behind while I go to California to wait for the call for a transplant. He has a great job that he enjoys. "No," he insists, "we will both go."

We will leave Juneau on the ferry. I've lost so much—my work, walking, running, hiking, back-country skiing—and now we are leaving our home. This is a place we fell in love with, the country and the people. Juneau is a vibrant community, filled with people passionate about work, politics, art, hunting, fishing, and their lives in this beautiful rainforest. We have both enjoyed our work here; I've helped wonderful Alaskan characters pass from this life, their family members now loved ones to me, people I embrace when we meet in the grocery store. Loren has managed a large, successful marine business and run a regional nonprofit agency. AD grew up here, explored the waterways and backcountry with us, camped on the glacier, learned to drive here, even broke a regional record in a high school track meet.

Friends are family here. With no road system and only boats and planes for access, friends really do become family. We leave them behind, friends we have sung and laughed with, friends with whom we have shared great joy and immense sadness. It feels like my heart is being torn out as we pull away from the dock. We take the farthest aft stateroom and watch Juneau fade behind us, consoled by the water and rugged coastline for this slow and painful process of leaving home.

13. LEAVING—*Then*

The *Sitka Spruce* was our second home, an old search and rescue vessel, with a sixty-five foot double-planked, mahogany hull. It was really a palace of a home after our tugboat. Very little rot. Right beneath our bunk, which had lots of sleeping space and very little head room, a large table folded down from the wall in the middle of the cabin. The tiny galley was just aft, followed by a shower on the starboard side and a small tool room on the port. The engine room, with two loud diesel Jimmies, was aft of all that, behind a hefty door that provided some level of soundproofing. Forward of the table was our son's room with four bunks just aft of the head. Two more bunks lined the sides of the table that we used for storing food supplies, books, and just about anything, including an occasional guest.

Upstairs in the wheelhouse is where we spent most of our time. There was a tiny wood stove, along with our large steering wheel and chart table. With windows all around, we had great visibility underway. Aft of the wheelhouse was a large deck and hydraulic crane we used for loading and hauling heavy items and equipment. We could also lash a large line to the crane's base, which enabled us to function as a tugboat. We didn't have a tow winch to haul and wrap the towline with. Either Loren or I were the winch, hauling in one-inch line, arm over arm, as we pulled in our barges. Far aft was a hold, a large open space we could use to pack fish.

The boat was AD's playhouse. He raced up and down stairs, hid in closets, and climbed up beside the radar to watch the water and weather when we were underway. His favorite toys were tiny rounds of wood he filled with hundreds of nails, skillful with the hammer, as he was with other tools and equipment. Hanging from the crane, a large, round, orange bumper served as his swing, capable of sending him out over the water.

Pulling away from the dock with the *Spruce* was a moment that completely thrilled me. I could never identify exactly why. As Loren maneuvered the boat out of its stall, I tossed off the lines and felt such satisfaction. Life became so simple. We had our entire home with us. We ate what we had or caught. We entertained ourselves and were surrounded by water and forest. And it was just the three of us—Loren, AD and I. We lived aboard our second home until AD was five years old, pulling away from the dock just about every week during the summer months, hauling supplies or barges to Forest Service camps.

There were a few summers when AD and I had to jump ship as scientists contracted with us to use the boat in Glacier Bay and Frederick Sound, to study whales. They studied ship sounds, trying to determine if the sounds affected the whales' behaviors. A playful or upset child onboard the boat would have interfered with the acoustical studies.

As we pulled away, perhaps it was the opportunity to look at Sitka from the channel that charmed me. We pulled out of Crescent Harbor, enjoying Sitka Sound, dotted with islands and opening up to the ocean. Totem Park was behind us—my favorite place in the world to walk, a pleasant path through the forest, with many totem poles. We passed under a beautiful suspension bridge as we headed into the channel. As we motored by the next harbor, we checked out the variety of boats. Some were caked with mildew, rust, or blue tarps; others were freshly painted, fishing gear ready to go. We never did much fishing, only a little packing. We had generous neighbors and plenty of fish.

Off our starboard side was downtown Sitka, the US Post Office being most visible, a great meeting place. The post office was followed by the Sitka Pioneer Home, with colorful, well-kept gardens, where I took my second nursing job, a job that I thoroughly enjoyed. Near the Pioneer Home was the Alaska Native Brotherhood Hall, where I learned about Tlingit dancing, storytelling, and art, and across the street, the Pioneer Bar, a frequent haunt of ours. On my parents' first visit to Sitka, we had a mix-up on times for their arrival, so Mary and I were down working in the harbor on a small boat we had purchased when they arrived. Mom and Dad had no clue where to go, as we had no phone. They asked the driver to take them to the Pioneer Bar, which they had heard plenty about. En route, the driver passed the harbor where we were working on our boat, and my folks spotted us. We looked up from our work to see Mom and Dad walking down the dock.

Across the channel, off our portside, we passed the Coast Guard Dock, Mt. Edgecumbe Hospital, and Mt. Edgecumbe High School. Alaska Native patients and students traveled from smaller villages in Alaska to both facilities. I worked at both the hospital and high school during the winter, walking across the suspension bridge to work. On clear days, the Aurora Borealis would still be dancing at 7 a.m., as the short daylight hours afforded longer dark skies.

As we motored north, we passed Sitka Sound Seafoods, where Mary and I broke crab legs and claws, and then we went by float planes, another harbor, and homes that dotted the waterfront. Sitka had seven miles of road in each direction, north and south. After that, and beyond the houses that hugged the shoreline, was the forest. The Tongass National Forest is the largest national forest in the United States, at 17 million acres. Named for a group of the Tlingit people, it is home to countless forms of wildlife, glaciers, rivers, peaks, and somewhere around 75,000 people.

Continuing northbound, we had a great view of Mt. Edgecumbe, a dormant volcano, as we rocked gently to the ocean swells. I felt as if the mountain watched over us all, especially as we left town on our boat. Before long, we were traveling inside waterways, the forested shore nearby on both sides. Maybe I loved throwing off the lines because I knew these waterways were coming. We passed by occasional boats, navigated currents and rocky areas, traveled with Dall's porpoises, watched eagles dive for fish, and saw an occasional bear on the shore. I was awed.

Always awesome, not always relaxing. We traveled in stormy weather, and even occasionally in winter storms. I recall questioning our work the year cold weather arrived early and either Loren or I had to get out on the bow and chop ice that formed on the deck. The wind whipped up the water, which landed on our deck and froze. It took a lot of work with the pickax to clear the deck, only to have it load back up within a short time.

Of course, there were things like engines, water pumps, generators, and plenty of other machinery that had to be working. Occasionally, they broke. When a water pump on the *Madrona* blew out in Sergius Narrows where currents ran rapidly, I was ready to abandon ship, intent on saving my unborn child. Loren jumped into the skiff and towed us to safety instead. One winter trip, when I leapt from our boat to tie it up at an unused cannery, three feet of new snow covered the dock. Unbeknownst to us, the snow covered a large hole in the dock. My jump took me dead-on into the hole. How I happened to land perfectly in the middle of the hole, falling straight through, I'll never know. I went right down into that water. I didn't land half in and half out, just right in. And I flew right back out.

Most of the time, our travels went smoothly. Rough or smooth, our young years together in that magical country have left us grateful and enriched.

14. MT. VISION—*Now*

I stopped taking walks because it got too cold in Juneau at my snail's pace. But now I'm at the start of the Mt. Vision trail, and I'm walking up, slowly. It's because my eighty-year-old father gets behind me and pushes so that I am able to go up the hill to see the osprey nest. This is California, not Alaska. I realize, ecstatically, maybe I can walk outside again.

We are staying with my folks in Inverness, a small, charming community in California's beautiful West Marin. Mt. Vision overlooks the town. Driving is something I can do; I am sitting still. Just can't run out of gas. I start driving to Mt. Vision on my own. I load my tiny oxygen tank on my back and take a step up the steep hill. I wait a few seconds and then take a breath and another step. I do this over and over until I am twenty-five yards up the hill. I turn and walk down, thoroughly enjoying that I can increase my pace. Downhill, I don't need as much oxygen.

I'm called back like a salmon to a stream. Day after day, I return, each day walking a little farther, winding my way upward. It's not wet and wild like the land I left, but dry, with thick, wild brush and madrone trees reaching out with their red arms. After two months, I am able to reach the end of the trail. The smell of the bay near the top is my reward for the effort. Here I rest and inhale the world. Downhill, my arms swing freely, and my whole face grins. Has life ever felt so good? In a few places, this winding trail looks out over Tomales Bay. In the same place each day, I watch a colony of ants whose life's work takes them back and forth across the same section of the trail. So busy, they are always removing dead ants. Am I more tender to all the death around me now that my own is closer? I greet them and walk carefully over their workplace so as not to add to their load.

In local shops and around town, I see people who look interesting. Should I try to meet them? "Hi, I know I'm sporting this oxygen and look like a very slow person, a sick person, but you might like me anyway." I never say anything, self-conscious about my infirmed state.

"So, Cathy, what are you doing these days?" those I know ask.

"Oh, the laundry." Or "Well, let's see. I get up and eat and walk a little, shower when essential." Showers are hard, taking too much breath. "I walk as far as I can up the mountain each day." That's my favorite. Quite often, I respond with, "Oh, this and that."

Mt. Vision helps me hold a sense of wholeness. My mind slips and slides around most of the time, living alongside this increasingly breathless body. I'm safer hanging out on the mountain than in my mind. Away from the mountain, I can develop a gaping, aching hole in my gut because I don't have an active life like I used to. Some days, it's as if I've been hit in my gut with a soccer ball. I know the feeling as I really did experience it years ago, when this body could still run. I tell myself, "Cathy, you are a child of God. You are your essence. You were never the other things you did; they were activities and work you did." I say these things to myself, but the ache stays when I don't quite buy it.

I don't have tea with God and Drie anymore. Drie has a new home. Her dander became too much for my desperate lungs, so she moved in with my sister Mary, to be showered with love by my niece, Maya. About a month later, Maya morphed from a youngster to a teenager, and Drie got dropped, no longer showered with attention around the clock. Mary came home from work, and Drie would look at her, give her a quick, irritating "Meow," and then squat and poop right where she stood. Drie was never one to tolerate anything less than complete adoration. A kind friend adopted her after that.

Although Drie is gone, it does seem that God is still around. God, still helping me to hold my gaze or bend my knee. I quiet my mind, and at times, I loosen the tug of all my thoughts. I realize, Hell, here I still am, without all my identifying claims to existence, and really, I'm still happy. I want to get up, walk up Mt. Vision, and spend time with my parents and with Loren. It's rich really. It's plenty. This is huge. My world is shrinking, but I am not.

My folks are a pair of honey bees, moving constantly from one sweet thing to the next, taking a walk or a swim at the beach, going to art class, serving on boards, driving elderly neighbors—who are a few years older than they are—to doctor appointments, shooting a round of golf, taking meals to seniors. The greatest gift in my life is their kindness. We live in two charming rooms below their home that were once part of their B&B.

When anger and fear rise in me, I can pour or pound my feelings out on paper or canvas in a wild and wonderful class where instructor Toni holds space for everyone. Wild Carrots. That's the class. On the day that I get up after a poor night of sleeping and try, breathlessly and unsuccessfully, to shower, I slam dark colors onto the paper. I move them around, slam some more, move and slam and move. I actually like the painting. It's dark, but that's no surprise. I create works of grief, of the dark woods I left behind, and pieces of celebration for the new woods I have found. Many dark paintings with bright windows or doors seem to emerge effortlessly.

Windows or doors to the other side? I don't know. We have moved here because I'm listed for a transplant in San Francisco, but I continue to harbor the hope for a cure, and to search for and chase down that one amazing California healer who will end this. Or perhaps my morning meditation will calm and settle me one of these days, so much that I will rise and be healed. I imagine it. I pray for it. Am I doing it wrong?

Even if I don't get healed, I am still torn about a transplant. Is it so wrong just to die? During my ten years with hospice, I watched plenty of people die who, I believe, were met by their loved ones who preceded them in death. I doubt it's too bad. And yet, my son wants to marry, and will he and his wife have children? I would be a grandma. Can I leave everyone I love if there is a way to stay around?

In my yoga class, I hold a pose too long and am severely breathless. How come? My oxygen was up as high as possible and I was doing so little. I lie on the mat for the remainder of the class, staying calm, trying to catch my breath. It is like breathing through a very small straw. A half hour later, class ends, and I am barely able to get up and leave. I remain terribly breathless. I know I can't panic. It will make things worse. I drive to the fire station a block away and sit there in my car for two hours until I feel like I can resume my day. I am a nurse. I know this is bad. I am far too shaken to cry. Am I ready to die? Am I ready for surgery?

Before I become severely short of breath, I spend time volunteering with the transplant donor network, and my heart gets cracked open by people I meet. This network is the organization that provides education and does outreach work, encouraging people to become organ donors. They have nurses who go to hospitals to talk with families of potential donors, very sensitively explaining what it could mean to donate their loved one's organs. This can be a difficult decision for family members to consider at times of such immense loss. Many people are waiting for organs. Many die waiting for transplant.

I meet a young woman in her thirties who will need lungs soon. Very soon. Young, not in her fifties like I am. And a young mother whose newborn infant died. She is working tirelessly, encouraging others to make the choice she made, to become donors. That ache inside me that worries about my own losses—it is moving over to make room for lots of folks I meet, for their pain.

Things are shifting as I sit to still my body and mind. I am being drawn out into this field of grief for these people I've met, and grief for those whose loved ones will die, making lungs and other organs available. I find myself sobbing, feeling the pain of someone who may give me their loved one's lungs. Day after day, I melt into tears. And I notice something happening to me. This sadness I am feeling is softening the fear I have of a transplant.

I hadn't really seen my fear until it softened. But of course I'm afraid. I've learned, as a nurse, what it means. I'll trade one set of symptoms for another, and we'll hope the second set is better. To keep me from rejecting the foreign body, the new lungs, I will take immune-suppressant drugs for the rest of my life. Rejection or infections, a balancing act. If I don't have enough medication, my body will reject the lungs. If I have too much, illness and cancer will be so much easier to contract. I will have to leave behind my natural, purist ways and take a whole slew of medications. "Just say yes," to whatever drugs I'm told to take. I will have to be careful to wash my hands often, avoid places where people have colds. Where will I find a place people don't have colds? Once transplanted, the countdown begins. Of those transplanted with new lungs, 50 percent will be gone in five years, and 90 percent in ten years. There is no going back. And I know the surgery is risky. My glued-up lung will have to be scraped out of its position for one of the new lungs to go in. I need to be at peace with not surviving. With dying.

In my dream, I am sitting at an outdoor church. It is empty except for my friend, Eileen, and me. A wild black stallion walks up to me, gallops off, lifting up into the heavens, flying to the moon and back, right back to me. This dream is so vivid, and it has taken ahold of me. I can't say just what it means, but it seems to offer the potential for transformation, a challenge to take a chance. I feel the power of transformation. Can I go under the knife and return?

No one ever cuts my curly hair well, but it's just a few days after the dream, and a woman in Inverness gives me a great cut. "I'll be back before my transplant," I tell her. "I'll need a good cut to last me some weeks in the hospital."

The very next day, I have an appointment with the transplant doctor. As I leave the hospital, I walk by this wonderful man whom I've met in the transplant support group meetings. I've been going to them "just in case." He was very ill, too ill to transplant, he had been told. Our transplant center tried anyway, and succeeded. He has a new heart. He is a kind, elderly gentleman full of appreciation for the gift of life he has been given. When he sees me, his face explodes in a smile, and his eyes twinkle as he says, "I've seen you at the support group meetings, and I don't understand why you aren't ready. You really look like you need new lungs. Do you not have someone to go into surgery with you? I'll go in with you, honey, if you want." I fold in tears.

Family and friends have been ever so carefully asking why I haven't gone active yet, when I am going to, would I please do it soon. Images appear—the donor family's grief in prayer, the stallion dream, the haircut, and the wonderful man with a kind, new heart. These are my signs. I know we all read signs the best we can. My son read his bear encounter as his acceptance, even welcome, by bears in the woods. Instead of going into the woods less or in a large, noisy group, he practiced his distance running alone in the woods. I might have read his sign differently. We each have the privilege of intuiting our own signs.

Loren and I talk. "It's been time for a while," we agree. We decide now is the time. I will let my team know I'm willing to be active on the list. I've been on the transplant list for three years, making my way toward the top. I am probably fairly high on that list now, which means a call could come quite soon once I'm active. Yet I've continued to say I'm not ready to go active, to be called in. They have been telling me I have a limited window. Certainly I don't want to have the surgery too early, while I still can use my own lungs. But if it's too late, my body's many systems will be too weak to handle the operation.

"You leave for Florida tomorrow, Loren. Shall we go ahead with this anyway?" We agree. He leaves for a conference, and I call my transplant team. I drive to Inverness to visit my folks from Pacifica, where we have relocated to be near to the hospital. There is no chance that I will get a call right away. Yet, I suppose it is possible, so I pack a bag for the hospital and toss it into the car. Toothbrush, hairbrush, book, drawings from the elementary school children.

When I arrive at my folks', I want to walk up Mt. Vision. Mom and Dad both want to go, but Dad offers to stay behind to watch my cell phone, just in case I'm called. The cell phone doesn't work on the trail up Mt. Vision. We take the leisurely walk, visiting neighbors we pass. It is getting dark as we return. Dad is pacing in the middle of the street. "The hospital, they called, you have to go in. You can't eat or drink." Thank God we took the walk. Otherwise, we'd be sitting before the fire with food and a drink.

15. THRILLED AND
TERRIFIED—*Then*

"This isn't one bit fun—not okay at all! We shouldn't be out here," I mumbled under my breath. Loren heard me.

"I know. We'll pull in to Chatham Cannery."

"That's a hell of a long ways at this rate." My tone implied that he was somehow to blame.

I was thrilled whenever we pulled into Chatham Cannery in flat, calm weather. We would set our table and chairs out on the back deck, relieved to reach our destination for the day. We would bask in the rare sunshine, stay out to watch the stars. Have a glass of wine. But when it was treacherous, I was not thrilled, and my tone of voice did it every time, implicated him.

I knew he felt bad when the seas were rough. He was the only true boat-guy in the family. AD and I were usually fine when running the inland waterways of Southeast Alaska, but outside on the open ocean, he and I took turns throwing up every twenty minutes into the plastic garbage can. On one such voyage, AD said, "Dad, why couldn't you be into something different, like airplanes?"

This particular night, we were traveling inland waterways in the *Sitka Spruce*, but it was rough out, and we had two barges in tow and were moving slowly. It was already dark, and we couldn't get to Chatham Cannery fast enough. We hadn't been moving as fast as we had hoped; we were in "the ditch," officially called Chatham Strait, a long body of water that gives the wind an opportunity to build over a very long distance. The wind churns waters beneath, whipping up waves that stack up one after another. And that's just what was happening. The stacking began before we could pull into a safe bay. It was starting to pick up, and visibility was poor. We did have radar, so we knew where we were, but I preferred regular old eyesight.

I walked out on deck to check on our tow. They were there, two small barges with small buildings on them, at the end of our towline, just as they had been all day. And the skiff … where the hell was the skiff? There was no skiff!

I scrunched up my face, as if that would make my eyes see further. I looked in every direction, as far as my eyes could see, but found no skiff. It had come loose. We had been towing it just a short way behind so that we could bring it alongside our boat and one of us could hop in and run it back to check on the barges. No short-tie skiff now.

"I don't see a thing except chop," I moaned, looking in the radar, seeing the screen full of the tops of waves being blown all over. Chop, the stacked-up, sloppy waves. Loren had more luck at the radar and identified a small spot some ways behind us. My heart started racing. This was not going to be good. I knew we'd be rocking and rolling all over hell and gone as we turned around to get the skiff. And then we'd have to get one of us into the skiff, and that was not likely to be me. And one of us would have to manage whatever the big boat had to do, and that was probably going to be me. Damn!

We circled back and located the skiff. Our sixty-five foot vessel and the thirteen foot skiff were both bobbing up, down, and sideways in the chop. We couldn't tie the skiff off short to the boat, as it was too rough and would likely break loose and take off again. Loren laid out the plan. He would jump onto the skiff as I brought the boat close; he'd have with him our large ring with four wires that attached to the skiff front and aft, starboard and port. I would operate the crane on our aft deck, maneuvering it over to Loren and the skiff. Then I was to lower it, and he would drop the ring into the crane's hook. All we had to do after that was lift up the skiff and load it on the back deck, keeping it from smashing into our boat or ourselves. That's all! We would place it along one side of our deck. There would be just enough room to settle the skiff down out of the way of the towline, if we snugged it right up next to the cabin.

I was shaking at the controls, but I knew how to run the crane, so I did. I couldn't scream and cry and run or fly away. Loren jumped aboard as I raised the skiff. It was a thirteen foot Boston Whaler, a fairly heavy skiff, built of fiberglass, with lots of extras we had added. As I lifted it up, that heavy skiff began swinging in harmony with the thrashing of the boat from side to side. Loren fended it off the *Spruce* as it came up out of the water, and then we got it high enough to bring it over the deck of the boat. It was swinging like crazy. Loren had to try to steady it while ducking to keep from being knocked over. My imagination started in: What happens when it knocks him over into the water, and I have to lower the skiff on my own and then find him, two barges in tow? And our young son? I quit that thought quickly. It wasn't an option. I'm sure Loren had similar thoughts.

It was an agonizing few minutes while the Whaler was swinging back and forth above the deck. As I lowered it with the crane, the Whaler would lunge at Loren as he tried to steady it. He would duck just in time. Lunging and ducking—over and over—before we landed it down on the deck and inched it to where we wanted it.

We tied the skiff securely, shut down the crane, and hurried back inside the warm cabin. AD, five years old, was still asleep.

16. GIFT—*Now*

To the family whose teenage son or daughter, brother or sister has just died: I am so deeply sorry for your loss. And given your pain, I am awed and grateful for the gift of lungs you have shared with me. Thank you so very much.

The phone call from the hospital doesn't get through to my father while Mom and I are walking up Mt. Vision. He's busy in the kitchen, and the cell phone is out at the far end of the living room. It rings and rings. The hospital staff finally calls Loren's cell phone, in Florida, just before he is to deliver a presentation. He calls my folks' home on the land line and reaches Dad that way. Five hours. That's all the time I have been active on the transplant list. I may have been uncertain about even having a transplant, but I have to admit that it seems to be falling into place.

Most people who have a transplant go through one, two, or three "dry runs." Two people, and sometimes even more, are called to come in when it sounds like an organ has become available. One of those called could be ill. Not a decent state to be in for such a big surgery. One may have a chest size closer to the donor's chest size. Organs may also turn out to be damaged, but just the possibility of lungs being available triggers the calls to at least two of us who are waiting and who are the same relative size and blood type. If we are not found to be the best fit, we are sent home. Or maybe we are a fit, but the lungs are damaged. We're sent home. Dry runs.

I am certain this will be my dry run, but I am nervous nonetheless. My folks drive me into the hospital. After thirty years of living in Alaska, the silver lining in all of this is having time with them. Now, here they are taking their little girl in for new lungs. My brother Judd, who is a take-charge kind of guy, comes to the city to wait with me in the hospital. He has a calming influence. Once I remind myself this is likely to be a dry run, sleep comes, despite the beeping hospital sounds. Awakened early by a nurse, I ask, "Dry run? Shall I go home now?" No.

Seven years after being diagnosed with LAM, I am wheeled into the operating room to have a double lung transplant. I overhear a conversation that is not meant for my ears, and I learn that the lungs I will receive are from someone who is sixteen years old. Oh dear.

I wake when the breathing tube is already out. It has been in for the nine-hour surgery and for some time afterward. I'm so glad I don't remember. Loren has flown home from his conference, without delivering his presentation. AD comes from Minnesota along with his girlfriend. She didn't think he should get on the airplane alone. Other family members gather, too. I am a mess. I feel horrible. My first words to Loren are, "Did we do the right thing?" He is devastated hearing my question. There is no turning back.

The first day, I beg and scream for something for pain. The surgeon, very bright and skillful, doesn't believe in using narcotics, wanting his patients to begin to breathe well right away. Narcotics suppress breathing, but I don't care. I want some anyway. There is a tiny needle in my back delivering something for pain, some medication besides narcotics. Things get better when we all figure out that the needle has come out. This same day, my first day, nurses get me out of bed to walk. I scream some more. "No! I can't!" They have me do it anyway. I recall another transplant patient, who, right after surgery, was so happy to breathe she jumped on her bed. I certainly could not do that!

I am desperate for oxygen as the nose-hose is removed and the oxygen is turned off. It is only the second day. The doctor explains that due to my poor lung capacity before the transplant, my breathing muscles worked differently, and I have to re-learn how to breathe correctly now. "It will come," he says.

"Please, please," I beg, "let me have the oxygen for just a day or two, even if it's just psychological." I've read about that, and I don't care if I need psychological oxygen. I really work on him. He goes over and turns it on, and I can't get that tube into my nose fast enough. "Thank you so much," I gasp and gush, nearly in tears. He has refused until this point.

Feeling more relaxed, when the nurse comes in an hour later, I tell him that the doctor has turned on my oxygen. The nurse walks to the oxygen meter at the wall and turns to me, smiling. He says, "Well, he did turn the air on, but not the oxygen."

I see imaginary mice on top of people's heads. I gaze out the window at a massive body of water that is spanned by a beautiful bridge, a city lining one side, and lush green hillsides on the other. "This is incredibly beautiful. Where are we?" I ask, forgetting I am in San Francisco and looking at the Golden Gate Bridge. My precious son insists on sitting with me through the night, in the dark, feeding me ice chips. The entire time, I wonder why in hell he and I are banished to a basement. I buzz the nurses to take me back to my room, only to learn I am already there. I am very confused, but I am breathing.

Before I withdraw from the intensely stimulating corticosteroid medication that was used for the surgery, I announce that I feel well enough to begin working out the very next day. AD and Loren look at each other and then back at me, nodding to humor me. As the days move on, and the drug withdrawal takes place, I grow horribly anxious, unable to call up any of my relaxation skills. I can't even meditate, something I have done almost daily for twenty years. I drive a few of the Intensive Care Unit nurses nuts with my anxiety—eyes wide, glued to the monitors to see if my heart is all right, if my oxygen level is high enough. Some simply turn the monitors away from my view. One decides I need something to put me out of my misery. After he medicates my IV bag, I am well on my way somewhere else.

I become certain they have made a mistake with my heart. I have been opened up with a clamshell incision, cut under my breasts from one armpit to the other, the sternum being cut and my chest opened like a book. I am bound back up with titanium, and I grow concerned that my heart is cramped and beating incorrectly. I tell the doctors and nurses that they have put me back together wrong. "It's tied too tight! My heart doesn't have enough room." Over and over I report this, to no avail.

It turns out my heart does have some issues. Just not the ones I think. I learn that I actually had a heart attack during surgery. When you think about it, my heart has been working alongside the old lungs for a long time, fifty-some years. I can imagine my heart may have been resistant to parting with my lungs. Surgery took longer than usual, as the glued-up lung was reluctant to come out.

Tubes are coming out all over my chest, draining the oozing from the cavity around my new lungs. Loren arrives early one morning to find me with breasts like blown-up balloons. At some other time, it might have been exciting, but in this instance a tube has plugged up inside me, and the fluid that should have been draining from my chest has found somewhere else to go. That same day, opening a get-well card from another woman with LAM, I read, "While you are in there, ask the doc and hospital to throw in a complimentary breast implant." The card opens to a pair of balloons.

Each day, I walk a little farther. I am becoming amazed. This has worked. I am breathing, and within a few weeks, I am on the stairwell. I have labs done daily to check the level of one of the three drugs I take to suppress my immune system. I must have X-rays and bronchoscopies. During a bronchoscopy, or "bronch," the doctors insert a tube into the lungs to look around. They can also insert fluid to wash out the lung. It's a lot easier to tolerate when medication is used that causes relaxation and amnesia. Not permanent loss, just enough to last during the procedure. While the surgeon looks inside my lungs during my first bronch, without any medication, I put serious dents into the palm of surgeon number two, who is holding my hand.

Mom and I are finishing up the last of my cold breakfast in the room when I get a glimpse of what I must have looked like the first week, when I was dragged out of bed, oblivious to the world. We hear someone walking up and down the hall, asking in a slow, limp voice, "Has anybody seen my breakfast?" After he's been by a few times, we look out, intending to tell him that we've probably eaten his breakfast. A nurse offered us an extra breakfast earlier. I am ready to offer to make a call for him. Leaning out the door as he passes, I see him leaning on his IV pole, full backside exposed. No, really, it's his backside and much more; his hospital gown is just barely hanging on by the neck ties. Oh God, I can't say a thing. We call the nurse. And then we giggle and shake with laughter. We laugh so hard we're crying. It feels so good. He does get breakfast.

Three weeks pass, and I'm discharged from the hospital. I was in intensive care for one week and then spent the next two in the step-down unit, a floor where I was still monitored closely, though not as intensively as the first week. Three weeks breathing. It's so incredible. I walk around the house just to walk around. How precious is this breathing in, breathing out! Such a gift I have been given! I am fantasizing about hiking, biking, cross-country skiing, partying, traveling. I am so deeply grateful for these donated lungs.

I take a handful of drugs intended to interfere with my body's natural response to these new foreign lungs. I understand that without these medications, my body would mount a massive battle to get rid of the lungs. Something I would not survive. One of the drugs makes me anxious, shaky, and delivers strange hallucinations when I close my eyes. I resist the urge to feel terrified, knowing that my transplant team is working on finding the right level. I won't have to experience this feeling forever. But I will have to take the drugs forever, or so I've been told.

I bolt awake at night, my heart racing, my whole body coursing with fear. Why on earth would I be frightened, now that I can truly breathe? I'm ecstatic to be alive, to breathe deeply enough to shower, do the dishes and laundry. Soon I will be walking along the beach, breathing in the salt air. Such a miracle! Yet I awake consumed with terror.

"Come see me any time," said the hospital chaplain when I left.

"I'll be fine. Thanks anyway," was my response. I change my mind. I'm going into the hospital often at this point, to have blood drawn to monitor my drug levels. I arrange to see her when I'm there but am feeling uncomfortable about this. I should be nothing but elated! I explain how amazed I am to be filled with breath, how blessed I feel about my new gift, and yet, I find myself waking up terrified.

"Your cells have been under attack," she says, "and your body, despite the new gift, has been mutilated." She explains that my cells may or may not know yet if this attack is all for the greater good. Of course. I'm both thrilled and terrified.

17. NURSE WALKING—*Then*

Loren and I did a fine job making the dream of sailing off into the sunset come true. Our thirteen years in Sitka were thrilling though it wasn't the sunset we sailed off into. It was the rain. Rain, rain, and rain. And I came to love it. Once I learned to wrap myself in rain pants, coat, and tall rubber boots, it rarely bothered me. And our boats afforded us warm and comfortable homes.

Sailing off was mostly done during the warmer months. I pursued the other dream I had during the winter: nursing. After leaving behind my initial job in Sitka of breaking off crab legs and knuckles, I began work at the Sitka Pioneer Home. There I met many old salts and sourdoughs, people who had weathered the rains of Southeast, the cold of the interior, and the storms of the sea for years. One resident had lived her adult life, along with her husband, in remote country with brown bears as frequent visiting neighbors.

After working at the Pioneer Home for a year, a wizened fisherman remarked, "You know, Cathy, you could get that smell out of your clothes with oakum." Oakum? Smell in my clothes? Oh my God, of course. As soon as he said it, I recalled noticing, just the day before, a nasty whiff from our bilge as I climbed down the ladder into the *Madrona's* engine room and forward to our bunk and clothes. Part salt water, part oil drippings, part lots of aging vessel. Yuck!

Of course I smelled just as everyone in my dock neighborhood did. We often sat with a cup of coffee on one another's boats, listening to the wind blow through the tall masts, rocking gently or not-so-gently to the waves stirred up by wind. Or we gathered on our large bunk forward of the engine to play guitars and sing. Certainly no one left due to the pungent smell. All our homes smelled the same.

I had been coming to work stinking for nearly a year? "Hang a strand of that oakum in your closet with your clothes," he said. I knew what oakum was. A bunch of strands of fiber saturated with a sticky tar-like substance. We pounded it between planks on our old boat when we hauled her out for maintenance and repairs. It kept water out. I went right out and bought some, washed all my clothes, and hung the oakum beside my uniforms, red flannel shirt, and blue jeans.

I worked for a few years as an obstetrical nurse, a few more as a school nurse for predominantly Eskimo students who traveled to Sitka for boarding school, and did a short stint as an emergency room nurse. After traveling to the Lower 48 for training, I opened a private practice doing acupressure, a type of energy work that involves using fingers on the same point system that an acupuncture practitioner uses. Even as I had the practice going, I continued nursing, dividing my time between the two.

I loved the choice I made to be a nurse. It was the hospice work that came later in my career, when we lived in Juneau that felt like the work I was truly called to do. In every nursing position I held, however, I thoroughly enjoyed my work. Many of my friends are nurses, and each of them feels the same way I do. It is often challenging, always rewarding, and the bonds we form with one another and with patients can be like those of close family members. Nurses don't fix or cure people; they support them in fixing and healing themselves. I love that.

The last job I took in Sitka was working with the Indian Health Service, a division of the U.S. Department of Health and Human Services. I worked with the program that was the first to be taken over by SEARHC, the Southeast Alaska Regional Health Consortium, a non-profit tribal organization of Native communities serving the health needs of Native people in the region. It was truly an exciting moment in history as the Native people assumed leadership and management of their own health care.

I took frequent trips, boarding a small plane in Sitka, to fly to Hoonah, Angoon, or Kake, all Tlingit villages of less than a thousand people. They might swell in size during fishing season, but I worked during the winter. The wind could be howling. Occasionally my trips were cancelled, but rarely. I would worry about flying in a small plane the night before I was to set out. After all, I had a young child and this was Alaska and it was winter, but just as soon as I was strapped into place, worry simply left me. What would be would be. I recall occasionally noticing that my pilot looked to be little older than a teenager. I'm sure they were older but not by much. On one trip to Hoonah, there was a very young man at the controls. After asking him how long he'd been at this work, trying to look casual and only mildly interested, he said, "I've been flyin' in Alaska for ten years now." How could that be? He looked all of seventeen. The wind was blowing like hell. "Hell, I'm not worried about this weather. We'll be fine," he assured me. The wind tossed us up and down and all over the place, and my unworried pilot clung to the bar above his head with a white-knuckled grip.

I traveled to these communities to teach health and wellness classes, mostly in schools. I learned far more than I taught, I think. I learned of the elaborate kinship system of the Tlingit people, of the spirituality and art that infused everything around them. During those years, I came to understand and respect a wholly different culture than the one I had lived in all my life. I learned to listen differently, to listen patiently, and to leave silent spaces during conversations. And I learned to walk differently.

It was in Hoonah that I learned about the walking. I usually stayed for five to seven days, and on one trip, I returned to my small hotel room after my first day in the community to find my pants all splattered with mud. The streets were muddy from the recent rain. The second day, I carefully observed everyone else walking in Hoonah, and no one had dirty pant legs. I walked with such caution the next day and the next, yet each time, I returned with very muddy pant legs. And each day everyone else was clean. It was not until the end of the week that I figured out why. It took me a whole week. My walking pace far exceeded everyone around me. What was my hurry?

The people of Hoonah had a pace of living I grew to appreciate.

18. AD's WALKING STICK—*Now*

Numbness is creeping up my leg, and I am overwhelmed by all of my physical problems. Too many, all at once. I'm not managing well. I can't stand this. My deep gratitude for another chance at living never wanes; still, I feel as if I cannot climb out of a hole that's smothering me. Right now, it feels like my problems will bury me. One foot is extremely weak, and both are partly numb; they have been for a couple of years. And now it's spreading up my leg. Neuropathy. I know I shouldn't be complaining, but I am. I feel rotten. I sport a brace for the weak leg, but I take nasty falls. Fortunately, I have only discolorations to show for it. I've just finished a year and a half of daily IV medication for a stubborn respiratory infection. I'm exhausted. The drug has zapped my energy and left pounding in one ear. "I think this drug is killing me," I tell the doctor.

"We have no choice," he says.

When I agreed to transplant, I knew I would trade one set of symptoms for another. I love breathing, and I usually love being alive. But right now I feel buried by hopelessness. I sit in the big blue chair in our home in Washington. We moved north from California for Loren's work a year and a half after my transplant. I am looking outside at the tall trees. I am soothed by their silent nobility. I am not sitting to be uplifted. I'm sitting to weep. So many setbacks, and now my feet are getting worse. I can't do all this. It's just too hard.

I melt into the chair, and the sobbing comes easily. It begins with tears, but soon my whole body is shaking, weeping. I miss being active. Grief and longing wash over me. I miss nursing. I let go. I can tell I'm traveling down that road to despair again, and I've learned that tears won't make it worse. Usually, they feel cleansing. I might as well let my sadness and grief have their time, or they'll just wait, nagging me for their turn. All I want right now is to be able to take a walk without falling down, move fast enough for my body to know it's alive. Is that so much to ask? I keep on sobbing.

As the tears and shaking at last give way to silence, there are the trees. They stand and wait. I love the silence and the space here with the trees. Crying has cleaned out my mind, and I see quite clearly that once again I'm feeling victimized: some awful thing is happening to me that should not be. I want what isn't.

My face may be covered with tears, but a slow smile happens. The smile happens when I remember—when I remember that I want to have what I do not have. Of course I do. It's so simple. And it's such a waste of what energy I do have. I need to remember this, the clearing out of my mind with the help of my tears.

A gift is offered into the silence, into this clearing: an image of AD's walking stick floats through my mind. My son loved to whittle away at wood when he was ten or eleven. Once he made a square with the inside carved out, leaving only a ball of the wood inside. He created a lot of things. He used to check the garbage can to be sure I hadn't thrown away "raw materials" he could use for his creations. He got mad at me one day when he found that I had thrown away an empty toothpaste tube. Raw material. The walking stick he whittled popped into my mind, with the comfortable hand grasp he had made. And the wavy lines he carved around the wood knots. I've kept most of his creations; surely I will have this one. We've moved six times since we lived out in the woods, yet, with each move, I think I've tossed in the stick among the rocks and shells AD collected, bringing them to the next home.

I can walk with his stick! Not only can I look forward to falling less often, I'll have my son with me on the walk! I am flooded with joy, astounded that, once again, I have been gifted with a shift in perspective. I cherish these moments of grace. Do the tears bring them? Do they arrive when I let myself drop into my grief? Shall I thank the trees? The silence? God?

I'm not sure what's more exciting—that I can walk with AD's stick, or that I have a shift out of despair, a change in perspective that has plagued me for weeks.

I head to the garage and rumble through shelves and rows of stuff. I find the stick. It feels solid and strong, infused with AD's presence, infused with grace.

I see that I can find my way home, to a state of joyfulness, to reunion with God, to what I consider holiness. I suppose that is what I want most of all. I want to walk and be well with fewer problems, but I think that, above all, I want to be at peace with what is. That is my greatest desire. Not just at peace, but joyful. Which isn't to say I don't enjoy being fit, feeling well. These things are simply not always playing at my movie theater.

An hour later, I return home after my slow yet pleasant walk. Today, I know, this is the way I walk. I learn to live with what is; I walk with AD's stick. I sit to read, pleased that I have shifted from despair to this flooding of joy.

Home alone that evening, I experience a sudden horrendous pain in my gut. What now? Haven't we done enough for today? Gas. It's one of the multitudes of things that seem to overwhelm me. But this is really severe. I try lying down, bending, arching, and nothing helps. Oh my God, now there are gurgles from my gut way up in my chest. This can't be okay. I call 911 and crawl in pain to wait by the door in my pajamas. Loren is at another conference in Florida.

19. FEAR—*Now*

You are still, frozen, but for the most miniscule shift of your eyebrow. You notice your mom and dad are not here. We were all kicking the soccer ball; now they're walking down the beach. It's just the two of us. We were laughing and running and jumping; we didn't notice. But now you notice.

Frozen with fear, not even able to turn your head to look. You did that before you froze, when you noticed them missing. I come to you, sit on the grass, offer Grammy's arms, my arms. No. Now your lower lip has a slight quiver. I will wait here while time and the world hold still. I will wait, hold time with you. My arms will wait.

Ever so slowly, you let me enfold you.

***

I understand what it's like to be frozen in fear like my granddaughter. I love when it moves aside to the arms that hold.

No sooner is my despair dissolved with the grace of a clear mind and my son's walking stick than my guts burst through a hole in my diaphragm that must be left from a surgery. The intestines are up frolicking with my transplanted lungs, a place they can do lethal damage. I am rushed to the hospital and into surgery to get them back where they belong.

It is odd to say, but I'll say it: I have a great time. The place of peace I find before being hospitalized carries me through the entire week's hospitalization. I had planned to campaign for the presidential election, instead of having an emergency surgery, so I do it from my bed. I ask everyone who comes into the room their thoughts on the election, if they are registered to vote. Despite plenty of pain and tubes, I really do have a good time.

I get another chance to stick around. I get to continue watching what the coming years have in store for AD, Elizabeth, and Clara. Each year I continue to live, I delight in watching my granddaughter grow, my son be a father. I can walk at dusk, watch the sun rise and set, and continue enjoying family and friends. I sit with Loren at the end of each day, glad we are both still here, and share the day's tales. Medical miracles and loving prayers have given me so much.

Despite fatigue from surgery, life is flowing easily. I've got the timing of my forty-seven pills down. I can't miss one and I don't. The medications keep me alive and they take a toll on many parts of my body. I see doctors for my lungs, heart, skin, eyes, and bones. I wear masks on airplanes or in crowded places during flu season. I protect myself from the sun with hats, gloves, and plenty of clothing. Loren and I have learned how to avoid people with coughs, to politely get up and move or leave a room. We wash our hands after touching door knobs or shaking hands. He gets a cold and is so careful I don't get one, despite my suppressed immune system.

Through all the medical treatments and emergencies, Loren has managed to stay connected with marine activities from California to Alaska. He's become a "boat-guy" who is very much in demand. His newest work is in both Washington and Alaska. We walk, breathing deeply and with gratitude, among the cedar trees in Washington. Four blocks from our home, a spiritual community opens their arms to us, takes us in, and loves us. And we love them. We are students and teachers to one another, whether in meditation, book group, prayer, soup kitchen, or worship. We hold and prod, comfort and challenge one another. And we laugh.

Waking up to breath each day, I live much like everyone else lives. Miraculous! To live and breathe. The nature of Loren's and my adventures has calmed, though we still seem to find opportunities to be thrilled and terrorized together. Just to make sure of that, we have squished ourselves into a small sailboat for trips in Washington, Alaska, and British Columbia, putting ourselves at the mercy of the sea. And our own common sense or lack of it. This, too, may just be the way the two of us walk.

I still get frightened, overwhelmed by complications, and yet it might be possible it takes less time for me now to "come 'round right." That's my phrase for shifting perspective, for standing and looking with different eyes at a situation that appears entirely too difficult. I had LAM and then a transplant. Yes, a transplant, a second chance to walk in the forest, drink tea with friends, enfold Clara or read her a book. Yes, a transplant; there will be issues. When I get long stretches of feeling well, I start to expect to rest free in the arms of life, without any further problems. I can be slow then, to turn around, to accept life as it unfolds, as it is.

After a sailing trip, my dermatologist says, rather frankly, "Your lifestyle doesn't fit your transplant status." I explain to him that I diligently protect myself from the sun and get my skin checked every three months. What could go wrong?

20. CANCER—*Now*

I sit on the edge of my chair, staring. Instead of doing what I plan to do at my computer, I look beyond, out the window, my eyes attracted to the delicate green leaves of a Japanese maple— pale green but bright, in contrast with the dark soil it sits in. I am restless, and I notice my breathing is shallow. I'm terrified. I know all hell can break loose with this tumor at any time. I knew darn well that my time would come after years of suppressing my immune system. I'm actually all right with dying. It's dying from a form of cancer that I've seen before, working as a hospice nurse, that doesn't hold any appeal. Would any?

A tumor that started two years ago as skin cancer on top of my head has invaded not only a node in my neck, but has spread well beyond. A few of my transplant drugs and sun don't mix. I've known I'm at risk for skin cancer, and I've covered and protected myself with sunscreens, hats, and umbrellas constantly since the transplant. Even sailing, I dress in clothes that provide sun protection, use face covers, hand covers, and even wrap myself in sheets, making certain that every inch of my body is covered. But I'm sure there are seconds, even minutes, I am exposed to the sun. I spent years growing up in California's sunshine and many more in Alaska working aboard our boats or hiking and skiing the backcountry. I couldn't, and I wouldn't, change a second of my life; my time is just up. I was angling for an avalanche, not tumors growing on my head and out the side of my neck.

A surgeon, who is truly a magician, transforms the top of my head, bringing up an artery and vein to cover the deep scar left when the rapid-growing cancer was removed. He covers the whole area with a thin piece of skin from my leg, a graft. Once again, I have a great time in the hospital. This time, it's because Bernice stays overnight with me. She has been my delightful friend since fifth and sixth grade, when she and I spent the night together each weekend. She moved away, then I moved away, yet we've kept in touch and now we live near each other again. In the hospital, we giggle as we did when we were young. I feel grateful, fears put aside thanks to my generous friend.

Despite the surgery, the cancer races on, filling up nodes in my neck and growing beyond them. It stays a step ahead of all our efforts. It is unwilling to respond to pleas, prayers, acupuncture, energy healing, qigong, imagery, and chemotherapy. It is bulging out the side of my neck, pushing into my throat, hijacking my tongue, making it difficult to eat, swallow, and to talk. Lightning bolts shoot up the side of my head.

I am gazing, once again, out the window at a beautiful tree. This one was a gift from my father. He's like that. Gardenias, plants, trees. And I'm sitting with hope. For what? Of course, I hope that suddenly the chemo, which hasn't worked, will change its mind. Loren believes it is just delayed due to my transplant regimen. He points out the chemo has to work its way around my many medications. I also hope that the new healer I have begun to see can work magic for the disappearance of the tumor and pain. I have been praying for healing, imagining myself well. That is my hope. I put my hands to my neck. Yes, it's still there, and no, it's not smaller. Yet.

Haven't I already done my sick time? Isn't losing my breath, undergoing a lung transplant, spending three of my seven years since the transplant taking daily IVs for infections, and four additional surgeries enough? I've lost enough! I've been diligent, finding my way to walking joyously even as life has shrunk, over and over. Maybe I will find my way, once again, to walk in joy, but now I'm in way too much pain. I'm too tired. I'm frightened and exhausted.

I've been here before, this place where I am consumed with fear. I feel as if a wave of disaster is hurling me out to sea. Where are those arms of God that can overwhelm the overwhelming? Arms I can rest in, that will assure me I will somehow be okay? How is it that I have lost my way again? Why can't I walk that way I want to walk—free of fear, accepting of what is? When pain and fatigue set in, the dark and ominous clouds of despair and fear seem to follow so rapidly. Down I descend into hell. Why can't I hold the clarity of spaciousness, of God, of presence? Please.

21. HATS—*Now and Then*

I am dressed in blue jeans and a boy's shirt, and on my head is a plaid newsboy cap. A pack on my back is filled with some of the essential things I'll need for a week's trip—at least—on the road. This is exciting. I'll hitchhike somewhere and see another part of the world. I'm a bit young for this kind of thing, but I think it will work out fine. I think my brother and sisters will miss me, but then again, I'm quite bossy, so maybe not. I'm sure my parents will miss me. I wish I didn't have to worry them.

This was a recurring fantasy I would entertain before going to sleep when I was a young child. My plan was complicated by the fact I was not a boy. I planned to manage that by tucking my long hair up under my hat. Because I was young, perhaps my girlish face could pass as that of a young boy's. I knew I wouldn't take this trip, but I loved to imagine it. I planned to get in that first car and take a ride to wherever the driver was going. I would find a place to sleep at nights and then get up and go to the next place. I didn't even think about what or how I would eat, or where I wanted to travel. I just dreamed of hitting the road.

When I woke up, often my thumb would be in my mouth. That's the same thumb I was using on the road. Too bad. My brother and sisters and I got stars on the chart in the kitchen each morning our thumbs stayed clear of our mouths. I often thought that, because I didn't put it there intentionally, only woke to find it in place, I could still report I had a night free of thumb-sucking. If I had enough, when the time came, I'd get to go to the zoo. I always got to go to the zoo.

The first time I found a hat like the one I had dreamed of, I was twenty, living in Ireland, studying theology and philosophy. Plenty of newsboy caps sat on the heads of elderly men and young boys on the streets of Dublin.

When I arrived in Dublin, I managed to find a flat but then did not manage the bath well. I took a cold bath, failing to discover the coin machine on the wall for hot water. Not interested in any more cold baths, and with a week until school began, I decided to use my thumb to explore the Irish countryside. I packed a few supplies in my small knapsack, found my way to the road out of Dublin, and headed out.

The driver of my first ride recommended I stop for a tour of a beautiful island set in the middle of a lake. When I arrived, I paid the small fee for the boat ride to the island, which was just a short distance away, covered with flowers. There, on the elderly boatman's head, sat not only a newsboy cap, but a plaid one just as I'd dreamed of when I was younger. That fellow and I had a hell of a time communicating, our two versions of the English language very different. I understood him just fine when he put his hand on my knee, and he completely understood my, "No!"

Over forty years later, the newsboy caps are worn by young and old, men and women. I wear a lot of different hats, but the newsboy caps are my favorites. They cover just perfectly the bald and scarred top of my head. I have survived this cancer so far. The two surgeries I've had on my head, each necessitating a graft taken from my leg, have left me looking like a Franciscan monk. I'm always a bit shocked when I look in the mirror, hatless. I simply cannot take myself seriously until I have one on.

I have a lot of hats. I can emerge with a bright red hat that will keep my head warm at subzero temperatures, drawing all the attention I might dream of. Bright, colorful, and twisted pieces of yarn scream out in every direction five to six inches. Another has a large crop of false hair on top just where I have none. So precious are those hats that friends have knitted for me. A few hats I've been given are marvelously exotic, something one might wear to far fancier places than I frequent. My niece, Maya, who has far more flair for elegance than I, tells me, "You must wear them."

"Where?" I ask.

"Just anywhere," she replies. When I explain to her that I can't possibly wear them along with my bulky, sturdy shoes, which I need for my unstable feet, she replies, "No one's looking at your feet, silly. Just tie a nice scarf around your neck and head on out."

I head out. No more hitchhiking lately, just a lot of heading out with a hat on. I've tried a wig, but when I wore it recently to the store, I returned home to find it had migrated sideways. I can only imagine what I had looked like. I wore it on the airplane when we went to visit AD, Elizabeth, and Clara, and when we arrived Clara took a look at me, went to give Grandpa Loren a hug, and refused one for me. I quickly replace the wig with one of my hats, and that did the trick.

I have tried to revive the art of thumb-sucking. Radiation and surgery have left me with more precious time to live, as well as a swollen tongue with a very painful sore on it. I need to keep my teeth away from it at night, and I think my thumb would be a perfect solution. All the childhood thumb-sucking led to braces, and now my mouth is no longer inviting to a thumb.

22. FLOOR CLEANING—*Now*

The fear and sense of dread and unfairness about this cancer is so great. I do my usual, watch the trees for a while and then hit the deck and weep. I work so hard at being positive. I am positive. I am grateful for all that has come my way. I busy myself holding onto that gratitude, cleaning the house, planning the meals, fluffing up pillows. I sign up to be of service. Anything but face this dread and fear. For what can it offer me besides the desire to give up? I push the pain and fear aside day after day. But today, I drop to the floor. I drop to weep, swept up in a wave of grief. There is nothing I can do.

Damn, it's dirty, this kitchen floor. I get up for a clean rag, soap, and water to accompany me in my despair. At least I can clean this weeping ground. So I sob, and I clean. Using only a little arm motion and scooting my butt along, I clean. Back and forth, over and over.

After learning from a doctor that my tumor will grow out the side of my neck, over and over I see it in my mind. Bringing it to mind now, I am horrified, and I actually scream. I revisit all the difficult and painful moments of the past, sobbing about each one. The glorious new life I was given seems lost to me now. Why did I make the choice to live on?

Back and forth. I could clean the floor with my tears. Back and forth. My thoughts slow down, and they quiet their screaming rants as I scoot my way from one end of the kitchen to the other. About halfway to a clean floor, I shout, "I shouldn't have this. I've had enough!" As soon as it leaves my lips, I am startled by what follows: that familiar smile. "Oh," I challenge myself, "are you so sure that's true? You've had enough and shouldn't have this too?" What is apparent and true is that I do, indeed, have this thing. So, I clean. All my years of pain and breathlessness aren't here right now. Nor is a big, ugly, stinking, and bleeding tumor that will supposedly grow from the side of my neck. It's only a small bump. It's just me, here, now, cleaning the damn floor. I can almost laugh. Chuckle is more like it. I can get so worked up going over and over the unfairness, reliving the difficulties of the past, building terror for myself as I imagine the future.

I drop into that space again, where all the worry bleeds out of me, and the tears cleanse my mind. I would really like to stay here, maybe even move in for good. This place where I sit in the present, instead of in tomorrow's terror. This is the way I want to walk, each day. How is it I get pulled so far away from the calmness of being present? Why can't I get upset, realize I'm disappointed with what's happening, and go immediately to a peaceful presence instead of taking the long slide down into hell first? I want to climb into my chariot and go straight to God. I know this peace and clarity I call heaven, or the arms of God, are present constantly, and it is for me merely a matter of turning or choosing, but I get so busy fighting off pain and terror of tomorrow that the choice evades me. Hoping for something different than what is happening seems to obscure my wholeness, to interfere with choosing heaven, of resting in God.

Speaking of God, I've been watching God most of my life. My earliest memories of being with God are in the old church back home. I would dress up in a flowery dress just like my sisters. Grammy made our dresses, and we wore hats and gloves to match. We would follow my mother, small ducks gliding behind their mum. I loved God.

In high school, much to the dismay of my poor family, I insisted that we all get on our knees every night to pray the Rosary. Kneeling at a bedside, repeating prayers to the Virgin over and over, we were often blessed with an unexpected surprise. Someone would slip up during a prayer, usually an intentional move on the part of my brother, Judd. We would start giggling, trying our best to continue praying, holding back the laughter. But when a giggle slipped out from my mother, or tears sprung from her eyes as she tried to them hold back, we gave in and collapsed, bent with tears and laughter. How could I not love God?

I maintained my serious gaze at the Divine. As soon as I got my driver's license, I would borrow the family car early in the morning before school, before my parents needed it, and drive to the Catholic Church to attend Mass. Confirmed in the Catholic faith, I took my enlistment in God's army very seriously. Though my noble deeds weren't much more than cleaning an already clean nun's convent, if that was the order, I was ready to march.

It was in college that I met an amazing and powerful teacher, priest, and professor of theology, which was my college major. I credit him with opening a new insight into God. He offered an unofficial class for theology students in a small basement room of his Jesuit living quarters. Week after week, together we searched our souls for purity, for a deep understanding of God. He called his course "Creativity." His ultimate challenge to each of us was to find within ourselves the ability to be completely present and spontaneous, freeing our minds of all concepts of right and wrong. We were fascinated, and it was difficult, at nineteen years of age, to imagine remaining free of judgment.

In Ireland, two years later, I encountered what I believe was divine intervention in my life. Traveling side by side with a big ex-con, I took soup and bread to those living on the streets on Dublin. Young college students, full of idealism, were paired with someone a bit more streetwise for nighttime duty. One night, the ex-con and I met a gentleman who ventured out on the streets on his own each night, separate from our school project. He was out in his van offering food, matches, and bandages. "You want to see my dream?" he asked me as we stood around a barrel fire.

"Sure," I answered, expecting a picture of Hawaii with hula girls or a fine, fancy car. The guy was working two day jobs, saving up for this dream. He carefully unfolded a large poster of a fully equipped ambulance, complete with ointments, equipment, and bandage wraps. He wanted to replace his van for traveling around Dublin at night with a vehicle that was well stocked to provide help.

My heart was struck. I dropped out of theology studies that next day. I knew without a doubt that God had knocked at the door of my scientifically-skilled mind. I started saving for nursing school. How do you argue with God?

I think to myself, as I sit on the floor, that God isn't anywhere to be found out there, but right here, and right here, again, the next minute. I believe I am offered the opportunity to know God each minute. Sometimes I know Him to provide solace or purpose, and other times, She is my source of creativity or inspiration. I just bring Her along. God, along for the ride. This thing, the next thing, cancer, a seashell being dropped onto the rocks from the beak of a gull.

As much as I hope and pray for a cure, forty years after studying with my theology mentor, I agree with his premise. Come to the moment open. Don't judge it. Take what it offers. Argue with what is, and I'll miss God. Hope for what isn't, and I will miss more. I have a tumor in my neck, and my floor is clean.

23. ACTUALLY—*Now and Then*

"The humpback whales you see in these waters travel the twenty-five hundred miles each year between nutrient-rich Southeast Alaska where they feed, and Hawaii where they play and mate. Actually," I continued, "there are a number of humpbacks that stay all year-round." This was part of my two-hour narration as a naturalist on large passenger vessels in Juneau, the same summer I would blow out my lung. I didn't realize how often I used the word "actually" until my sister Carol was visiting. For much of the trip, she was screaming ecstatically as the whales were bubble-net feeding. Eight whales would circle below and around the perimeter of a large school of herring, releasing air bubbles that rose, encircling the school of fish with a curtain of bubbles. And then, suddenly, all eight of these forty-some-ton mammals rose to the surface, jaws wide open, swallowing the herring and water in a huge gulp. Sinking back underwater, they would strain out the water through the large baleen sheets inside their jaws, leaving the tiny fish inside for a meal. Screaming gulls feasted on the herring that flew out of the water.

When Carol wasn't excitedly watching and screaming, she was listening to my narration. It's the "actually" I found out about after the tour. My sister is observant and kind. Very tactfully, she mentioned, "You use the word 'actually' a lot. It's okay, but you might want to use it less."

"How much too much?"

"About every other sentence, at least." At least? Oh my. I just couldn't imagine she was right, as I'd been doing this for over a month already. But as I started in the next day with my 150 passengers, I noticed she was right.

"Actually, actually, actually." Actually, it occurs to me I use the word a lot.

I became lost when I was diagnosed with Lymph-angioleiomyomatosis. Not just from the diagnosis and symptoms, but from the crash my life took. I was someone doing things, going somewhere, building a name for myself in my career, and I had a decent income. I had lots of friends and a hardy, Alaskan, backcountry body. In only moments, the ground was pulled out from under me. All those things I thought I was, no longer defined me. I lost my ability to be productive and to do the things I loved.

Actually, it wasn't quite like that. Though it took me many tears and screams on slow walks among the trees, and along the waters of Lynn Canal, I began to do some reframing. Hadn't I been given a grand challenge to prove the experts wrong, that I wasn't growing a "terminal" illness inside my lungs? I understood the power of the human body and human mind; I could reach inside and find the skills, find the healing needed, and the cysts would shrink, and the disease would disappear. I would focus and pray; I was a healer for others, after all. Hadn't I been given a great challenge?

Actually, I wasn't able to chase off the illness, to find the healing of my physical body that I sought. Despite my efforts, the cysts continued to accumulate in my lungs, and they continued to burst, leaving me short of breath. I lived in terror of a repeat of the first time my lungs blew out, when I was rendered breathless, not merely short of breath. I lost the fight, lost more and more of the things I was able to do, and I lost self-esteem as I continued to decline. Despite meditation, chi balancing exercises, yoga, healing practices, and care of my body, I grew more and more breathless. I lost too much.

Actually, I'm not so sure. Was it really too much? I grew. I learned to drop into an empty space of God, not the space where I ask of God and get or don't get something. A different space. God, where there is room for all things. Room for my failure to heal, room for being overwhelmed, and room for me to grow. Hadn't I offered in prayer I was ready? And asked for a sign that I would be okay? Hadn't I been given one when the bird touched down on my chest? Yes, I knew, I would be all right, I was all right.

Actually, over time, I forgot the power of that moment. As my breath grew fainter and fainter, I grew anxious and angry. How could I possibly be okay if I couldn't breathe? Oh, I know—believe me—that we all have to die. Heavens, I'd been a hospice nurse for nearly ten years. Of course I knew, dammit. I'll die. That's how I would be okay, if there was to be no breath left. Yet I struggled. I didn't want to die. In isolation, I watched as the world went right along without me.

Actually, Loren inhabited this landscape with me. We walked it together. I would lose my life, and he would lose his wife and partner of many years. When I got chest pains, when my lungs collapsed, or I coughed myself into a weak blob on the floor, his chest hurt too, and he became breathless. Together, we held out hope, on one hand, and on the other, we were coming to terms with death. He taught me to loosen hold of my expectations, to take each day one at a time. He didn't tell me about these things. He just did them.

We were disappointed, sad, and overwhelmed and yet, actually, we deepened in our appreciation for the preciousness of our lives, the preciousness of one another and of our son, family, and friends. We began to move through our days differently, with enhanced reverence, aware of the poignancy of the present, of the quality of life moment by moment. We learned to give over to God so many of those things we thought we had control over. I found that every time I lost something, there was a way to turn, and turn again, to come 'round right. Though I lost my identity as a healthy woman, athlete, nurse, adventurer, and traveler, I was still whole, and the "what is" was enough. As my breath declined and the circle of life I inhabited grew smaller and smaller, there was still room for joy.

Actually, quite honestly, I'm still working on coming 'round right.

24. WHY ON EARTH AM I STILL HERE?—*Now*

Most days I do okay, but not today. It is nearly six months since I finished radiation for the cancer. "If," the nurse had said, leaving a long pause after saying it, "you do recover your strength, it should be in about six months."

"It won't be an 'if' for me," I responded. But was I right? The six-month mark is just around the corner. Will I magically feel better in two more weeks? I eventually responded to the chemotherapy—and responded well. The doctor and I decided to try radiation. Maybe I would be in that small percentage of folks for whom this cancer could be cured.

"You seem to be working the second you get up and then until just before bed," I nag Loren. "It's hard to do anything fun together."

"But really," I mumble to myself under my breath, "let's be honest, Cathy." I'm hardly ever feeling well enough to join him.

Eventually, it hits me: "Of course," I say out loud, which I do so often if no one is around, "why on earth would he want to be around me?" I lie in bed as long as possible. Then I toast a few pieces of bread, scramble some eggs, and make some tea. Nauseated all the time, I stare at the food for a while, beginning to pick at my food as Loren is finished, and I'm still eating as he showers and is out the door. Then I take the twelve pills that go with breakfast, choking on at least two. I drag myself though the dishes, stopping to check e-mail, pick up something on the floor, look out the window awhile, and then consider a shower. An hour later, I emerge from the bathroom, ready for a nap. Some days, I get out and do things; others, I don't. I'm obsessed with the news, listening over and over to what's really pretty much the same thing. "CEOs have increased their profits by 57 percent, and child hunger is up by 33 percent," is my greeting to Loren as he walks in the door after work. Or, "There goes anything you have invested for your retirement."

The poor guy has been living with his time-bomb wife for fifteen years. Why haven't I just died? Five to ten years, they said. We've had wonderful times. I was present when AD married, have fallen head over heels for our granddaughter. We have returned to Alaska many times, and I have been blessed to wake up to a new day, a new cup of tea, and the beautiful Pacific Northwest day after day. Yet, now, many days are like today and yesterday, with low-grade nausea, hours spent trying to eat, dragging myself around as if I'm a hundred years old.

"I'm doing fine," or "I'm great," I say when asked. All things considered, like the fact I should or could be dead, I guess I am doing great.

I try to get a walk most days, work my way through exercises that build my chi and do a little stretching. Is it helping? Am I really supposed to be here? On the days I feel awful, I seem to have amnesia for the better days. I sink, and I can't climb back out, can't recall what it's like. Discomfort and pain seem to be accompanied by illness in my mind. I know this is depression, yet when I have days of feeling better, when the nausea passes, or a headache or severe neck pain is gone, I will not even remember how to find the depression again. Not that I want to.

Who in their right mind would do anything differently than Loren is doing? He has been the most patient, loving, and kind companion one could imagine for this difficult, life-changing journey. He never complains, believing that setting expectations for how life should be delivered is no way to live. He lives with what arrives. And works. And works.

I'm broken beyond my ability to put the pieces together at this point. I can't seem to blow energy into myself. I can tell I'm not as sharp as I used to be. I watch myself speaking at times, and dull things come from my mouth. I cry because of the nausea and pain, not to cleanse my mind or to shift my perspective. I can't rekindle the fire. I just want to fold up into the earth, the dark earth, deep in the forest, and let go. When asked if I'd like to take a walk by someone, my response is often, "Oh, I enjoy being alone, taking a walk by myself, hiking alone." It's true, I do like it. It's also true because I don't have the energy to interact with anyone. Alone is easiest.

Right now, I give up. I don't have answers. I don't know where God is. Probably not interested in walking with me today.

25. MT. MARATHON—*Now*

"Why," I was asked, "is grieving holy?"

"It's holy because," I hesitated, trying to find words to explain why I had named the workshop, Grieving, a Holy Journey, "it just is. How could it not be?" This was opening day of the loss and grief group I facilitated. "Every inch of life is holy. And grieving someone or something that has been loved and lost can be a tortuous journey through fire. The fire burns us until there is nothing left but ashes. And there, in the ashes, we rise again, transformed by our love and loss, and by the fire itself. Sacred. Holy."

That was before the cancer. I have dropped back into the darkness. I am buried in the ashes. Radiation flattened me. Despite being certain I would stay strong and fit, jogging each day of radiation treatment, instead, I lay in bed or stared at the wall, nauseated, vomiting, and listless. Getting to the car and down to the radiation room was my exercise. I haven't been able to slam the door on the thoughts and feelings of despair yet. You might think by now I could. I've had practice, learned to turn myself around, but I'm dragging here. I sure as hell have learned, however, that I am in charge of ushering depressing thoughts back out the door. "I understand why you came; now you can go." It is so incredibly difficult when I hurt or am nauseous, as I am so often. And yet, difficult as it is, it must also be simple. They are thoughts. Let them go. Or feelings. Move them along. Simple.

Almost eight years since the transplant, I have found another mountain I can walk up called Mt. Marathon in Seward, Alaska, where Loren works in the summer. Seward is on the southeastern tip of the Kenai Peninsula, three hours south of Anchorage, accessed by the Seward Highway, which runs through country that is so exquisite that when driving alone in the car I simply scream with delight. Tall mountains rise up from the water. Beluga whales are occasionally seen, shimmering on the surface of the water, and despite my eyes being on the road last time I drove the highway, I spotted a mountain goat perched just off the road on a steep rock cliff.

Seward is a small town at the head of Resurrection Bay, which empties into the Gulf of Alaska. It is a charming town with a lot of hotels and restaurants, stores selling clothing, crafts, art, candy, yarn, and more, ample services for the thousands of summer tourists and its year-round three thousand residents. My favorite haunt is the bookstore. Boatloads of visitors travel out on sightseeing vessels each day to see humpback and orca whales, sea otters, sea lions, puffins, and steep cliffs where kittiwakes make a summer home. This area, where glaciers pour into the sea and mountains reach up to the sky, is part of Kenai Fjords National Park. Hundreds more visitors head out on charter fishing vessels to catch salmon and halibut. Seward is home to the Alaska SeaLife Center, a state-of-the-art wildlife viewing and research facility. As I write, employees are caring for a baby walrus whose mother died in northern Alaska. She can't be left alone and wants her head on a lap when she's awake.

Each year, Seward hosts the well-known Fourth of July Mt. Marathon Race, on a trail that heads straight up and straight down. AD ran it a few times when he was in Fairbanks for college, describing it to us as "insane." Hundreds of men, women, and teens run the race, many returning bloody and exhausted. A few are hospitalized.

A bar-room wager is said to have initiated the event eighty years ago. "Do you think anyone could get up to the top of the mountain and back in less than an hour?" That's my mountain. And for me, it is a marathon of a mountain to climb. I have found a trail that's easier than the runner's trail. It winds its way up, but it's still very steep in parts. I've decided that I will work my way up as my rehab program for recovery from radiation, which has left me without much muscle mass. Ten minutes the first few days, twenty after that, and longer as I am able. I'm slow, and we may leave Seward before I reach the top. It has become my metaphor for the marathon recovery this seems to be. So has Resurrection Bay, because I seek resurrection on these days I can no longer find joy.

I continue to imagine and nurture the hope of miraculously being free of pain and illness. More honest with myself, I know I need to stay in the present moment, letting the past and future recede from my thoughts, no matter what tidal wave my body is riding through. I am not succeeding very well; I get lost in the pain. I don't like what's up for me now but I believe I can still find my way home to a peaceful mind. Problems aren't easier. I've just learned to trust I can get home. I can choose home. God's arms are not missing. I am God's arms, voice, hands. It's up to me.

Illnesses, along with accompanying thoughts of despair, are things I can mistake for being who I am. I am not my problems, my successes, or my story. "I am riding through all of this, whole, healed, complete," I tell myself. Yet, easily I can sneer in response, "Oh sure." I get stuck to my thoughts. At times, I can un-stick myself with far greater speed than I once could.

I fell on my steep Mt. Marathon hike last week. I was up to about an hour on the mountain. The bruise I got from the fall is easier to heal than the bruising I do to myself when I get stuck to my thoughts of fear and despair. For five days this week, I felt too ill to go anywhere, a great time for the onslaught of feelings and thoughts of worthlessness, fear, jealousy, and anger. Still, after all these years, "No fair" creeps in.

On my hike, I find a hole in the forest to crawl into. I'm drawn over and over into the darkness of the forest. I'm surprised to learn it doesn't invite me to give up, to nestle in to die. Instead, the cold earth and knotty roots are God's arms; I am comforted. I let go and unhook from despair. Over and over. "Shush," says the earth, followed by, "soften that thought." Eventually, I grow quiet. I'm not worth less or more. I just am. Still, I'm a mess physically. "Shush."

It's almost time to leave Seward, and I haven't reached the top, but I suspect the mountain will be here next year. I might too.

26. NOW

In a cave behind a voluminous waterfall, Kenny and I watched in awe as the cascading water roared only inches away. We worked hard to get there, swimming against the power of the falls and clawing our way over the rocks. Thrilled, we wondered if we might live in that place forever. I was sixteen and awed. Kenny was attractive, and the falls were breathtaking. Together, we felt the magic that our newfound vantage point afforded us, a secret place from which to look out at the world.

As my body slowly returns from being wasted by radiation, food is becoming enjoyable again. And I feel a life force pulsing through me, the hint of a thrill at being alive. The fire in my belly is being rekindled and I'm amazed. I know that it can all change in a moment. And will. After all this training, I am ready to commit to living in a place like that magical cave from my childhood, a kind of seat for my soul. From this seat, I will have the vantage point from which to watch the events of life cascade before me, and be awed by the magic and wonder of a life that is at times filled with laughter and purpose, and at other times, full of pain. I commit to holding my gaze on grace, where I can watch my life's unfolding, with a "Yes" to everything than tumbles over the falls. All of it? How could it be otherwise?

I'm thinking about the commitment I made just hours before my lung blew out fifteen years ago. And St. Anna whose help I invoked. She is said to have prayed for years and years. That is the guidance I have learned to take from her. To pray. For years and years. As I retreat into prayer and stillness, I can soften into the seat of my soul, that magical, often evasive cave of God, instead of tumbling, clawing my way upstream in the falls. And soften into being enough. I understand by now that the disappointment, even despair, will likely come along when pain and illness are overwhelming, and that finding my way home may elude me. Only for a while, I hope. I really do want to rejoice in all of it. Right up until I'm finally finished.

I have enough experience with others who have died to know that I shall have no trouble finding my way as I shed this body. Dying has drawn so near already. I know I will miss life as it slips away. That's part of the blessing of this ride I've been on. I've come right up to death's door, and the gift that it offers is the preciousness of living. Should this be my last round, I will give thanks to all my loved ones who have cascaded over the falls with me in my theater or supported me from my soul's vantage point. To Loren especially. You have held firmly to the present, with what comes along, not grasping after what you had hoped or planned for. And to my parents, who prayed and prayed, and who have traveled with me on some of the more horrendous rides. I am sorry you had to watch your child suffer. That's hard. I think your gift of seeing a glass half-full at every turn is working its way into me. Thank you. To my siblings, how much I have appreciated you, there at every turn. My heart runs over with you as I feel you with me always.

So many friends have tumbled over the falls, willing to jump into the rough spots. Together we have traveled, explored the wilderness, climbed the mountaintops, or slept on ferries. And then, there you were, traveling to care for me, patching up holes, coaxing me back to life, pouring me into cars, tricking me into eating. Letting me weep. Thank you. Thank you. Bless you.

And to those I worship with at the Suquamish Church, I delight to be among you. You have been my partners in keeping the flame of passion for the Divine alive. You have held me as I held you. Together we have peeled away our stories to find our truest selves and taken a stand for a just world.

I began putting stories together with the intention of leaving them for then three-year-old Clara. Who knows, I may be around to tell them to you myself, Clara. To her father, my son, I delight in countless memories. My favorites might be of romping in the wilderness with you, fondly recalling times you would stop, awed by the beauty around us, at the way a ray of light broke through the trees, or at the power of a storm. You would beg me to leave the trail and really explore. You had and have a spirit of wonder all your own. How much I love you is indescribable, something you know about now as a father. I am proud to be your mother, and I continue to delight in you, in the way you live in awe of both your family and your work. You have a beautiful woman to walk beside you and a spirited and charming daughter to keep you filled with wonder.

I am deeply appreciative of the medical professionals who have had my back throughout this ride. My gratitude is boundless for the family that I don't know, but who gave me the gift of life at a time when they lost a loved one. Thank you so very, very much. I cherish your gift.

I bow to Mother Earth, blessing you for the dark holes I have found to rest in, the mountains I have climbed, your waterways I have traveled with Loren and AD. Your landscapes have infused me with powers of stillness, rootedness, wildness, and freedom. I am smitten with your many trees. So many have listened to my woes, drained my anger, and replenished my strength. I have been nurtured well beyond my greatest dreams by your wildness. Your forests, with room for darkness and decay, as well as light and growth, inform my soul and shape my prayers. I end on bended knee, humbled by and grateful for the fullness of life.

FOR FURTHER INFORMATION

The LAM Foundation urgently seeks safe and effective treatments, and ultimately a cure, for lymphangioleiomyomatosis (LAM) through advocacy and the funding of promising research. We are dedicated to serving the scientific, medical and patient communities by offering information, resources and a worldwide network of hope and support.

Visit the website for information or to donate at www.thelamfoundation.org.

Second Wind Lung Transplant Association serves the lung transplant community with a mission to improve the quality of life for lung transplant recipients, lung surgery candidates, people with related pulmonary concerns and their families, by providing support, advocacy, education, information and guidance through a spirit of service, adding years to their lives and life to their years.

Visit the website for more information or to donate at www.2ndwind.org.

8505396R00085

Made in the USA
San Bernardino, CA
13 February 2014